How child grow

Forthcoming

2 from three to eight
3 from nine to adulthood

How children grow

1

from conception to two

Mark Lovell

Routledge & Kegan Paul   London

First published in 1975
by Routledge & Kegan Paul Ltd
Broadway House, 68–74 Carter Lane,
London EC4V 5EL
Set in Imprint
and printed in Great Britain by
Ebenezer Baylis and Son Limited,
The Trinity Press,
Worcester and London
© Mark Lovell 1975
No part of this book may be reproduced in
any form without permission from the
publisher, except for the quotation of brief
passages in criticism

ISBN 0 7100 8093 X (C)
ISBN 0 7100 8094 8 (P)

Contents

Foreword by Dr Hugh Jolly		vii
Introduction		ix
Chapter one	In the womb	1
Chapter two	From birth to one month	10
Chapter three	Early feeding, and the mother-child relationship	20
Chapter four	Up to six months	39
	Some questions that parents ask during their babies' first year	46
Chapter five	Personality development	49
Chapter six	Moving around and walking: up to one year old	62
Chapter seven	Speech	69
Chapter eight	The second year	79
	Some questions that parents ask during their babies' second year	90
Chapter nine	What can go wrong?	93
Chapter ten	How thinking develops	106
Chapter eleven	Two years old and beyond	115
Further reading		129

Illustrations

Diagrams

1	Stages of growth	22–3
2	Breast-feeding: typical pattern of supply	25
3	Eye and hand	44–5
4	Social development	54–5
5	Stages of walking	64
6	Play development	114

Tables

1	What can your baby see?	12
2	Babies' growth: weight and height	24
3	Feeding	26
4	Social progress (up to 1 year)	53
5	Personality development according to Freudian theories of infantile sexuality	61
6	Learning to walk and run	62
7	Growth of speech	77
8	Immunization	96
9	Immunization programme	98
10	Problems you should take to your doctor	99
11	Social progress (1–3 years)	117

Foreword

Yet another book on child care! This could be the reaction to this new book, but it would be wrong because there is so much for parents to learn about how their children grow that there can be no limit to the number of worthwhile books on this important subject. And Mark Lovell's book is certainly worthwhile.

Bringing up children is much more fun if parents know something about normal child development. Discipline becomes more understandable and less of a problem, while the whole process of being a parent creates less anxiety.

It's a good idea to keep a Baby Book provided it is filled with the right sort of record. No longer should it contain dull and old-fashioned facts like weight and the amount the baby ate but it should comprise descriptions of your baby's increasing skills. Normal babies develop at different rates and it is fun to compare succeeding children's progress and, with increasing skill as a parent, to watch for the early signs of each new area of development. In this way you will have no difficulty in accepting that no two babies develop at the same rate. A baby cannot progress at the same speed on all fronts at the same time. You may have one baby who talks early and walks late while the next one does it in the reverse order.

Many of a baby's movements in the first three months are automatic (reflex). A newborn baby will 'walk' when held upright with his feet touching a flat surface. This reflex disappears after a few weeks and normal walking, sometimes called the 'second walk', will not appear for some months.

Until he is about eight months old a baby has no idea what has happened to a toy he has dropped—it has dropped out of his world. But then he begins to follow it down to the ground—an exciting new stage for you as well as your baby.

This book will help you to know whether your baby is developing normally and to learn how you can help him. A baby is very responsive to everything going on around him; he is naturally friendly and would be unable to imagine that anyone would be cross with him.

Of all the signs that he is developing normally, curiosity is one of the best and should be encouraged. For this he needs his mother's time most of all—time when she plays with him and talks to him. Special 'educational' toys are not necessary but understanding his next stage of development and helping him towards it are essential.

For example, it helps to know about the oral phase of development (p. 58). A child should not be discouraged from putting things into his mouth, provided they are not so small as to be swallowed. This is the way he explores his environment, so obviously it is crazy to block the entrance with a dummy! Moreover, a dummy may cause him to spend longer in the oral phase of development instead of moving normally on into the next stages described in the book.

Understanding the development of a baby increases the close relationship between a mother and her baby. Such a mother will be armed against the nonsense and old wives' tales she is bound to hear such as 'you will spoil your baby if you pick him up too often and then he will dominate you'. A normal baby can't be 'spoilt' by a normal mother—you will only be enjoying each other more.

And now I hope you will enjoy this excellent book.

Hugh Jolly

Introduction

This is the first book of a series that has been designed to explain how children grow in more detail than is usually found in books of 'helpful hints'. Of course this is ambitious—because there is so much about the development of the body and the mind that is still imperfectly understood. But at least one can draw parents' attention to some of the main issues involved. In this, I have tried to avoid insulting parents' intelligence, by delving rather further into both physical and psychological processes than is usually prepared for a lay reader.

I believe that parents nowadays are impatient with authorities of one kind or another who communicate with them only at a superficial level, on the grounds that a little knowledge might do more harm than good. They want to know more, and the success of specialist magazines, books and consumer groups reflects this demand.

There are two impressions I want to avoid. First, this book cannot be considered in any way a substitute for qualified medical advice. Second, while I draw readers' attention to experimental work that helps explain children's development, I trust they will not regard this as a spur to experimenting with their own children. The objective is that they should observe their children with more understanding, not with the spirit of the laboratory.

My own discipline is psychology. For information on the physical side of children's development, I have had to rely on doctors and physiologists, whose help in advising me on what to read, and in subjecting what I have written to very careful scrutiny, I gratefully acknowledge. On the psychological side, I have been influenced by a large number of people, whose help has also been invaluable. I cannot mention them all, nor the clinics, and the many parents and children who consented to give me interviews. But I must give special thanks to Dr Norman Dixon, who has helped me steer my course through some very complex waters.

Mark Lovell

Chapter one

In the womb

At birth, the average baby is nine months old. Babies do not appear punctually on the dot, and appearance at any time within two weeks either side of the expected date is perfectly normal. A baby appearing a little outside these limits is not necessarily at any disadvantage, apart from causing his parents some concern.

The precise calculation is this:

(a) Work out what was the *first* day of the expectant mother's *last* period   1 January
(b) Add 280 days to this date   8 October
This is the day he is most likely to be born (in Leap Year 7 October).

Adding on 280 days is the equivalent of adding on nine months plus seven days. The seven days allows for the time taken up by the last menstruation, and for a new ovulation to have taken place. Fertilization of the new egg is considered to have happened at any time during the subsequent 'fertile period'.

But babies are no respecters of dates. Some will be premature and some will be late. In many cases, where the mother's period is light, or variable in onset, there is uncertainty about when the last period began anyway. It is worthwhile trying to forecast when the baby will probably arrive, but it must be recognized that this is a very inexact science. All kinds of factors may influence an early birth, or a late birth: some are hereditary, some depend on the state of the mother's health and what she has been doing, some are directly concerned with the growth and positioning of the infant, and some are psychological—that is, the mother's hopes and fears can influence this too.

The description that follows is of a baby whose life in the womb goes right through 'to term'—that is, he is born when he is already nine or close on nine months old, and his development is normal for that length of time. Very late births are rather rare nowadays, since they are artificially speeded up if there seems to be a danger to the infant or his mother. But premature babies are always with us, and they will be discussed towards the end of this chapter.

The baby starts as an ovum, or egg, that is fertilized. It attaches itself to the side of the womb, where a placenta develops. This word means 'cake' in Latin: it is the complex of tissues which grow with the egg and contrive to feed it, and mediate its blood supply during pregnancy.

Once the egg is fertilized, it has received everything it requires to determine many of the most important characteristics of the child that it is to become. Assuming that conditions are in its favour, and that it grows according to plan, nothing else can affect it that will change its sex, or the features of its mother and father that are being passed on to it.

When a human being is conceived, each cell of the new living being contains 23 pairs of chromosomes. These pairs consist of one from the father, and one from the mother. Each time a cell divides (which is the way that growth happens) the chromosomes in the newly formed cells are replicas of those in the parent cell. This procedure makes certain that a hereditary tendency does not get 'lost' before birth, or later. For the chromosomes contain molecules called genes, which are the essentials of what gets handed down.

But *what*, exactly, gets 'handed down'? If child development were totally a question of genetics, this book could be a good deal shorter. The fact is that although some of a child's features are obviously hereditary—his hair colour, perhaps, and its thickness, the colour of his eyes, and the tint of his skin, and so forth—there are others which are very much a matter of dispute. What about quick-temperedness? Or intelligence? Or talent at football or music?

The best answer is that these kinds of trait—whether they are classed as 'personality', 'intellectual' or what-have-you—are probably partly hereditary and partly a question of how the child is brought up. This includes questions of influence on him as well as of what kinds of attention, rewards, and punishment he is given. The kinds of trait that are very obviously hereditary can be divided like this:

(a) Simple physical features (colour of eyes, etc.)
(b) Complex physical features (height, etc.)
(c) Comparative sensitivity to different kinds of stimulus (sharpness of sight, keen hearing, sensitive fingers, etc.)

All these can be easily demonstrated as running in families. Less easy to be precise about, but very likely, are family differences in the formation of the brain and the rest of the central nervous system. Degree of control over temper, over hunger, over reaction to pain may be transmitted in terms of differences in the chemistry of the brain that are determined genetically. But how this control (or lack of it) is *expressed* by an individual child may owe more to what he is made to believe his parents will like, tolerate, or cut short. He may, then, have in his genetic make-up a certain *predisposition* to be like this, or like that, but whether this effect on his personality grows, or is blocked or disguised, is very much up to his upbringing. Nervousness in children can start with a predisposition: it may develop when they sense that their mothers are nervous, or if they are made anxious by unreasonable demands. A nervous child can also be one who has no such predisposition—but has been under considerable stress.

One final point is worth making about heredity. Research work by Sheldon and others has shown that there are personality types corresponding to 'somatotypes'—that is, the build and shape of your body. This fact, taken together with the evidence that complex physical features are transmitted genetically, suggests that personality can at least to some extent be transmitted in the same way. But how much is transmission, and how much of Sheldon's evidence reflects the way the fat people and thin people think and behave just as they are expected to behave—is very much open to debate.

The child begun in the womb may, of course, be twins, or several children at a go. Twins may be 'identical' or 'fraternal'— depending on whether they originate as one ovum which divides ('identical') or two ova which are fertilized at or near the same time. Identical twins will always be the same sex, while fraternal twins *may* be of the same sex. Multiple births invariably involve more than one ovum.

Despite being of very little weight during his first few weeks in the womb, the baby can cause dramatic changes to his mother's appetite, digestion, and well being. This is despite growing slowly in size—reaching about half a pound in weight only towards the end of the third month—and adopting a fixed position (the 'foetal position') in a kind of crouch, which is unvarying during this time.

Many babies do not, in fact, get further than this. Excluding those cases where a miscarriage is deliberately procured, it has been estimated that 15 per cent of pregnancies end in miscarriage. This happens usually between the sixth week of pregnancy and the end of the third month. There are many reasons why a mother may miscarry. Her hormones, or the structure of her womb and the neck below it, may be unsatisfactory for allowing the foetus to get established strongly. Otherwise, accidents, or poor diet may increase the chances of miscarriage. A frequently-heard comment when there is no obvious explanation for a miscarriage is that 'it's as well it happened because there must have been something wrong with the baby'. This is no doubt often said to comfort a discouraged mother-to-be, but it often has truth in it as well. For example, rubella (or German measles) is known *both* to increase the chances of miscarriage and the possibility that her child will be mentally handicapped, when a woman gets it during the early weeks of pregnancy. There may be a number of more subtle problem situations that affect pregnancy in a similar way, and are difficult for medical science to detect and isolate.

Assuming that the foetus negotiates this difficult time, its chances of successful birth increase markedly from the fourth month onward. This is the time during which it is acquiring distinctly more human characteristics, and individual ones at that. In the fourth month, hair starts to appear. Some, admittedly, is formed on other parts of his body than the head, but this early head covering usually remains until shortly after birth while the rest is lost before birth except with very early premature babies. Also during this month, tiny ridges of skin begin to form on the palms and the fingers. Even at this stage, every single foetus has a distinct *pattern* to these epidermal ridges—just as every adult has a different set of fingerprints.

The foetus' growth has depended exclusively on the supply of blood and nutrients from the placenta through the umbilical cord. This continues, but now the foetus starts to swallow some of the amniotic fluid (the 'waters' in the sac which surrounds it). This develops in a way that is important later: after birth, the baby will need well-structured rooting, sucking, and swallowing reflexes when he is fed.

Although the mother is well aware of changes in her body during this time, it is usually only in the fifth month that she feels definite signs of life in the child himself. What she feels is a movement of the foetus in the womb. It is certainly not a big movement, but the surprise element may make it seem like one. Mothers describe this first movement in different ways: 'a shift', 'a tremble', 'a flutter' are examples. It is usually felt about two weeks earlier by those enjoying their first pregnancy. Typically, this will happen when she is four and a half to five months pregnant.

The foetus has always had in it the makings of a heart. But it is only now, when the mother is five months pregnant, that a doctor will expect to be able to hear the heartbeat with a stethoscope. Ultrasonic listening equipment has been used to pick up indication of heartbeat much earlier.

Between the twentieth and thirtieth week the first shadowy movements turn into a long series of movements. Not every baby becomes a real 'rambler', as some doctors describe a baby who seems to change his position every day or so. The popular idea that 'I am feeling him kicking' is not always accurate: what is often felt is the sudden pressures of a general movement against a part of the mother that feels sensitive to it.

All this time, the baby has been in his half-inverted 'foetal' position. Gradually his head, arms and legs have begun to make little movements towards, or away from his standard position. The arms get more early 'exercise' in this way than the lower limbs. Consequently, the legs and leg muscles are relatively under-developed at birth.

It is not unusual for a mother to get very little 'kicking' indeed: this need *not* mean that there is anything wrong with the baby. It may be solely a matter of her internal geography. Some babies, who have been 'kicking' lustily, stop this days before birth. This is no cause for alarm.

Some of the hand movements late in pregnancy seem very precocious indeed. In the ninth month, the fingers can grasp the lower lip, and a kind of sucking takes place.

Throughout pregnancy the baby usually moves frequently into and out of the position that is normal for birth. This means having his head down, with his face turned inwards. A common alternative is to have his head facing outwards. Less common is for him to be in the 'breech position', in which his bottom is poised above the birth canal. There are, of course, other possibilities, but they are progressively less usual as the date of birth draws near.

About the early part of the ninth month, most babies have established themselves in the direction they intend to take. There they wait until birth. But they can nowadays be turned, if a doctor decides this is the best thing to do to avoid an awkward delivery. This means manipulating the baby from the outside so that he goes round the womb. As he is very well protected in his amniotic fluid, there is usually no danger in this at all.

The normal baby will be born, then, at nine months. He is likely to weigh about 7 to 8 lbs, and to measure 20 inches from crown to heel. He is chubby—largely the result of a rapid increase in putting on adipose tissue during the last month. This helps him to survive temperature changes without undue discomfort in the first few days after birth; and to pass through the brief period of weight loss, which immediately follows birth. He will lose as much as three to five degrees of body temperature as soon as he leaves the womb, because the ratio of his body surface area to his weight is now bigger than it will ever be later in life. The 'brown fat' included in his addition of fat is an important insulator.

Some parts of his body are much more developed than others. All his muscle fibres are there: they merely need to grow. The face and heart muscles are well advanced. His fingernails seem remarkably well advanced—and may even need immediate cutting to avoid self-injury. The bones of the inner ear are nearly adult size. But teeth are (usually) absent—a good six months away. The stomach size is minute: it is going to have to increase its size three times over in the first month. His bones are spongy, porous, and flexible. The spinal cord could be bent like a half circle. He has, in fact, *more* bones than an adult at this stage: because many of these fuse together as he gets older.

Parents sometimes wonder how a newborn baby can *breathe*. While in the womb, the trunk and diaphragm muscles have been expanding and contracting. This exercise is crucial, because big contractions are needed to fill the lungs with air. The muscles have to work hard: they produce 42 breaths a minute, compared to 12 for an adult.

Just occasionally a foetus survives the danger period for miscarriages, and continues developing for a while inside his mother's body, but then dies. A child born after the 28th week of pregnancy, who does not show any sign of life whatever, is technically called 'stillborn'. Prior to a stillbirth, a number of different factors over which the mother has virtually no control (e.g. her illness, or chromosome defects in the baby) may contribute to the foetus dying. This can happen several weeks before delivery, or at any time right up to labour itself. Stillbirths are comparatively rare.

When the 'average baby'—if such a creature exists—has been in the womb for 40 weeks, normal labour begins. But many babies are born before this. The reasons are clear sometimes, but are generally obscure. For a baby to be 'viable', with a good chance of surviving, *both* his weight *and* the time he has had to develop seem to be important. The two factors are closely interlocked. For example, a baby weighing $5\frac{1}{2}$ lbs or less at birth is called 'premature'. But at any weight from this down to about $2\frac{1}{4}$ lbs, the chances of survival and of avoiding permanent damage are greater with every week he has spent in the womb. This is the concept of 'small for dates': a baby who is technically premature (in terms of weight) but has taken longer to appear may catch up with the others of his age group relatively easily. But a premature baby who has spent *less* than the average length of time that babies of his birth weight have been in the womb will generally find progress more difficult.

Even so, since doctors have recognized the basic needs of a premature baby—an atmosphere that provides oxygen, warmth, and humidity—and since science has been able to supply suitable incubators, and methods of feeding such children, the chances of their doing well have increased greatly.

About one baby in twelve is born prematurely. But of these, about one in three is 'small for dates'. And a good few others are twins. Since the presence of twins and other 'multiple births' can be spotted well back in time, good precautions can be taken in advance to protect the babies.

Some extremely intelligent and very successful and happy people were once premature babies. If you have a premature baby, this is a perfectly possible outcome for him. But there is evidence that if you take a very large number of premature babies, and compare them later in life with many who went 'to term', you can see a tendency for the premature to continue to be smaller than the others through childhood; to have a slightly lower average IQ; and not to do as well scholastically. The evidence is complicated by the fact that certain very different circumstances tend to go with premature birth:

(a) Physical: drugs and illness with adverse effects on the baby;
(b) Physical: fall, or other accident;
(c) Social: economically under-privileged parents, conditions.

Obviously if being premature were the *sole* reason for being less bright in the classroom, it would be necessary to accept that the social environment does not affect this. But it is well established that the measured intelligence, particularly when the measurements have an academic flavour, clearly favours upper- and middle-class children. The issues are so interwoven that it is only safe to conclude that in some cases, premature birth (especially when it is associated with possible abnormality or damage to the baby at or before birth) can be an indication of low achievement: but it by no means necessarily points in this direction if other factors are not pointing this way too.

Premature babies have to receive special care. Modern maternity wards usually have a 'prem baby unit' attached. Hospital policy varies on the question of allowing his mother to have access to, and involvement with a premature baby. It is important to a mother not to feel left out of the action; and this is important to the baby, because it affects her confidence and her relationship with him. Health considerations allowing, the aim should be to encourage maternal contact, as if at home, not separation, as if in a laboratory.

Recently there was interest in reports from South Africa that administering extra oxygen just before and at birth seemed to have a positive effect on a normal baby's progress. When reported in the press, it appeared almost as if some wonderful brainfood had been found, which would guarantee a race of super-intelligent children. What it does in fact, seems to be to reduce the risks of anoxia—insufficient oxygen—at this crucial time. Normally, extra oxygen is by no means essential, but occasionally it could help. It is true that the brain is the part of the baby's body that is apparently going through an important growing stage during the last days before birth. At birth, the weight of the brain is usually about 10 per cent of the total body weight—as opposed to about 2 per cent in an adult. This might lead one to suppose that if this process could be helped, great intelligence must result. But there is not nearly enough evidence that it can be helped artificially, from the outside—beyond the very simple level of protecting the mother and her infant. Those cases where super-children seemed to result from the oxygen treatment can easily be explained by the fact that greater interest was being paid in what they were doing. Babies like that, and respond to it.

When they are born, the vast majority of babies nowadays are healthy, normal, and eager to take their place in the world. But a very few are not, and for a complete picture we must consider them.

While they have developed better standards of medicine and hygiene for the protection of pregnancies, human beings have sometimes made tragic mistakes in the way they treat themselves and their environment.

Several substances are recognized now to have an effect on a baby. Some other things increase the likelihood that he will be born with jaundice. If a mother is exposed to too much irradiation, by X-rays, the chances of leukaemia or other childhood cancers are increased. If she takes excessive doses of vitamins, this causes a baby to develop the wrong sort of vitamin balance: whether the results are very serious or not depends on which vitamins were involved. Then there are all the illnesses a mother can contract while carrying her child: German measles in the second or third month of pregnancy is well known for being linked with mental subnormality, and deafness, in the baby, but other infections involving high temperature are suspect too. Much of this is a matter of sheer accident.

There is also venereal disease, cigarette smoking, and drug addiction. Syphilis is transmitted as congenital syphilis. Drug addiction may lead to drug dependence in the baby. Heavy smoking increases the chances of stillbirth, and is associated with children having low birth weight, and remaining smaller than average as they develop. As human beings do more to themselves and to their environment, they influence the development of their young in more complex ways. The more drastic results of pollution of the environment are well known (e.g. mercury poisoning leading to 'Minemata' disease in Japan, and affecting the children of those who develop it with cerebral palsy): many less dramatic pollution effects probably exist, but are too bound up with other factors to be pin-pointed.

It must be repeated, that although the things outlined in the last two paragraphs undoubtedly happen, they are *rare*. A normal person, with anything like normal care and luck, should not have to worry about them.

Chapter two

From birth to one month

Babies are born, survive, and thrive. However, at birth, the human baby is distinctly less capable than many newborn animals. He is not completely helpless, but he needs a lot of help. The behaviour that he can manage to produce is very limited. It takes him a long time to achieve the agility of movement, or the range of self-sufficient and self-protective acts that, say, a young chimpanzee soon masters. He needs greater care from his parents, if he is not to hurt himself, and if he is not to suffer from exposure to a hot or a cold temperature.

Some protection, all the same, is built into his system. Much of his mother's resistance to illness is passed on to him. Before birth he had the advantage of receiving his mother's antibodies into his own bloodstream. From about two months onwards, he will be able to build up his own antibodies. But meanwhile he may also have received further help in resisting infection if he has been breast-fed—both in the colostrum (the rich fluid that his mother's breast provides for a few days, up to the time that her milk supply is fully operational) and in the milk itself.

The human baby is also liable to be more in need of special care because of the fact that medical science has helped bring many babies to term who would have perished in the womb during more primitive times. There are also many more premature babies born, and since we now understand them and their needs more fully, they contribute to making the human baby seem particularly vulnerable.

There are many different forms that prematurity can take. Just as an older child may be ahead of his age group in some respects, and behind in others, so a newborn baby may not be uniformly at the stage of development to be expected of him in all respects.

For example, about one baby in three appears rather yellow at birth, through a touch of jaundice. This is more common among premature babies, but is by no means exclusive to them. And yet in itself it is usually a sign of prematurity of a particular kind. At birth, most babies' livers are sufficiently well developed to cope with the removal of a breakdown product of normal red blood cells, which has a yellow pigment. Other circumstances may have contributed, in any specific case, but the main factor involved tends to be the preparedness of this part of the child to help keep his blood stream pure. In most cases, it is simply a matter of waiting. The baby needs to take in a fair amount of fluid, to allow the cycle to establish itself properly; and the liver has to reach the stage where it can be efficient.

Underlying the problems of prematurity, and of being premature in some ways more than others, is the whole principle of maturation. A baby *learns* many things: but learning a new thing depends on whether the right parts of his brain and the rest of his body are *mature* enough to cope.

There is one basic reason why a baby cannot be helped to rise up on to its legs, like a calf or a foal on its first day of life. This is that the central nervous system, like the liver in a jaundiced baby, has not become sufficiently mature. This is part of the human equipment that is growing—increasing its size, its flexibility, and its functions, for a long time. We are talking about the brain, the brain stem, the spinal cord, and the countless cells, nerves, and connections between them that are within these, or form pathways between them and the sources of sensation—hearing, sight, touch, and so forth. Some parts of the system (mainly the 'primitive' parts of the lower brain, and what is associated with them) are comparatively well advanced in a newborn baby. His ability to smell and to recognize smells depends greatly on this 'primitive' part of the brain, and is practically ready to be put into use. It will be refined, of course, and his developing brain will help him build up a complex set of associations between remembered smells and other memories. But it is already well ahead of, say, perception of pressure on different parts of his body, and digesting the implications of this information for controlling and moving his limbs.

When a baby is born at term, and assuming that his development so far has been uniform, he has a certain number of acts that he can perform that are reflexive. This means that they are not really under his control, and they appear in his behaviour as responses, each to a particular stimulus. Some French workers in this field have estimated that a baby is born with approximately fifty reflexes.

Nearly all of these reflexes seem to have some kind of survival value: that is, they can help keep a baby protected, or help him thrive. Not everyone agrees on what constitutes a reflex, but the description of Brian, one week old, is of a perfectly normal baby.

Brian

When he was born, he started crying. Nobody knows exactly what prompts crying. Later, it will be varied to indicate hunger, discomfort, fear, and even just plain boredom. Brian's voice reaches a variety of pitches, and he produces different levels of noise. But it is always just crying. It is a response to a complex of feelings that all is not perfectly well: it is not really a preparation for talking, except in the very simplest sense that it contributes to exercise the right muscles.

Brian's eyes do not see much of the world about him. Accurate study of his surroundings would involve his being able to control his eye muscles, and to focus properly. During his first few days, Brian exhibits what is called the 'doll's-eye reflex'. If you turn his head when his eyes are open, you notice something slightly disconcerting if you are not expecting it—his eyes are slow to turn in alignment with his head. It looks almost as if his eyes—like a doll's—respond only to gravity. By the time he is two weeks old, this will have disappeared, showing that he has gained experience in using his eyes for looking and watching (see Table 1).

Table 1 What can your baby see?

At birth	Eye reflexes
	(a) pupil adaptation: the pupil contracts when light gets brighter, expands when the light dims.
	(b) eyelids close to protect eyes against strong light.
	(c) phototropic: head and eyes tend to turn towards (moderate) light.
	(d) 'doll's-eye' reflex.

From birth to one month 13

	Learns to focus eyes, but only on objects about one foot away.
	Learns to follow movement (for a short time) within this range.
1 month	Learns to focus on objects within a wider range.
	Watches mother's face (and exchanges looks) when feeding.
	Blink reflex, at sight of objects moving towards him.
	May squint at times.
3 months	Playing with fingers (and *watching* them).
	Observes new activity in any part of the room.
	Moves head round, to improve observation.
	Learns to look at what he is holding.
6 months	Can watch complex movements (e.g. of budgerigar in room) intently.
	Notices objects within range, and reaches for them with increasing accuracy.
	Unlikely to squint, if eyes normal.
1 year	Has learnt to use his eyes to look for something he has dropped.
	Can use his eyes to judge how to pick up small objects between finger and thumb.
2 years	All-round improvement especially at:
	(a) noticing small things and small differences;
	(b) judging movement and speed;
	(c) noticing obstacles.
3 years	Learns to distinguish colours, letters, pictures of common objects, and to match objects.
	Uses eyes to fit objects together.

If the light is suddenly switched on, he will close his eyes—a protective reflex. Similarly, he blinks at a sudden loud noise, and if his mother touches the bridge of his nose. If it is day-time and the curtains are gradually drawn open, Brian can be seen turning his gaze towards the window (that is, towards light), and if you look carefully you can see that his pupil size is getting smaller. Draw the curtains again, and his black wells expand. Turning to light, then, and adapting to light, are already part of his repertoire.

He can perceive comparatively little, however, because focusing is so difficult for him, and because it must be hard for him to 'organize' what he sees into something meaningful. This can be shown very simply. When a coloured ring is passed across Brian's line of vision, during his first week, it catches his attention only briefly. He cannot follow it with his eyes for more than about a foot. But by the end of his first month, Brian is following the ring much further. He still loses it if you move the ring too quickly. But during these four weeks his eyes, and the back part of his brain (where sight is 'organized') have made very considerable progress. This shows how much Brian had to learn when he began his journey.

Even so, he does not react much, even at one month, to objects which come towards him at speed. Not even a blink. This seems a distinct gap in his armoury of natural protection. It is probably because it takes longer for him to learn to recognize distance cues, than it does for him to spot movement. As he doesn't move around much, there is no reason why distance cues, or learning about perspective should play much of a part in his life. What is important to him is close at hand. He has to become curious about more things—in his second or his third month—before he will notice that something is coming towards him fast.

(In the Introduction, I noted that experiments with children are best left to medical and psychological researchers, who know exactly what they are doing. This is worth repeating at this point: there is no point whatever in trying to repeat what has been described above, only to risk frightening a baby.)

Like many other babies, Brian sometimes has a slight squint. He doesn't squint all the time, and he doesn't do it for very long. The two sets of his eye muscles are probably not developed to the same degree. This is expected to correct itself as the muscles get more practice, and Brian finds more and more interesting things on which to focus his eyes.

Brian's two favourite accomplishments are rooting and sucking. He is naturally able to deploy his lips the right way round a nipple or a teat, and once he gets the stimulus that all is set, he shows he can suck too. This is reflex behaviour. But although Brian requires no preparatory learning to be able to do it *at all*, he may take some time before he is entirely efficient, and adapts completely to the shape of his mother. This is worth a more thorough discussion, which is taken up in the next chapter.

One of Brian's more curious reflexes is called the Moro reflex, after the man who first studied it. When Brian is held with his legs and middle supported by one hand, and his head supported by his mother's other hand, suppose that she suddenly lowers, by a few inches, the position of this other hand. A young baby's head is too big a weight for it to be controlled by his neck muscles. It drops back and down as the support is withdrawn. When this happens Brian raises both hands upwards, cries, and stiffens his shoulders. This can be interpreted as a primitive piece of behaviour that might have served in a former era to keep hold on his mother, or a part of a tree. *Or*, it can be explained as having had a survival advantage by virtue of being a signal that baby is in trouble. Whether a 'biological' explanation of this kind is justified, or it is just that human beings develop that way, this reflex has been found particularly useful by doctors who want to check on a young baby's development. Brian reacts exactly as described above, with his hands responding in a symmetrical way. Variations on this complicated response can mean a lot to a paediatrician.

Brian's hand is very sensitive to the touch. Two major reflexes are very easy to provoke and to watch. Countless mothers, in fact, have studied both of them without having the slightest awareness of the physiological principles. When Brian's fist is clenched, a touch on the back of his hand will stimulate it into coming open again. If his mother puts her finger, or a spoon into the middle of his palm, Brian automatically grasps at it. This is reflexive at *first*: but he soon learns that his mother likes it. Because mother and baby enjoy each other's enjoyment, Brian learns to anticipate her finger by making graspings when he is looking at her face, before she has actually bent down to him. He also learns to hold on: reflexive holding soon becomes conscious holding, because Brian finds he can prolong contact with his mother in this way.

Brian's grasp is not the same as an older baby's. The object he holds is *in the palm*, not between palm and fingers, as will be seen at about three months. Grasping something between fingers and thumb comes much later still. But his grasp is very strong for all that. Some American investigators in Ohio measured the strength of many young babies' reflexive grasps with a dynamometer, and turned up a 'champion' who could exert a force of practically five pounds per square inch.

He also does various things with his feet. For his first few days, when touched on the sole of his foot, he jerked his big toe outwards. But very soon this gave way to turning his toes smartly downwards, as if grasping for what had dared touch him. This is a preliminary reflex pattern turning into something more mature. Another foot reflex is a kind of automatic walking. When Brian is held upright above a table, so that his left foot touches the surface, his right foot immediately comes forward. When this touches the table-top, the left foot marches on, and so forth.

This might be thought to be a basis for learning to walk. But in fact it seems to have nothing to do with *real* walking. For this, Brian's nervous system is not nearly ready, to say nothing of the muscles he needs to use when balancing. This walking reflex only lasts with him for a month or so, disappearing long before he draws himself up, stands, and tries to move along the side of a cot. Why, then, is the reflex there at all? Some relate it to a primitive level of development, suggesting that it is a survival from a progress pattern of one of man's ancestors. This is not easy to visualize as a theory, and the reason for the reflex's survival is not explained.

Brian can hear sounds perfectly well, although he cannot differentiate much between them. The sound of his mother's voice, and of other adults by association, is sometimes enough to stop him when he is crying gently—provided he is not 'well away' and very hungry. Loud noises alarm him, while a strange noise can intrigue him, so that he stops what he is doing and seems to attend to it.

Probably the most notable changes in his life pattern over the first four weeks are the way that he gradually shows signs of being able to move his head, as he spends less and less time asleep. Brian's head, at birth, is only about two-fifths the size of his father's: but the proportion of his total body weight that is taken up by his head is greater now than it will be at any other time of his life. It takes a lot of effort to start manoeuvring it around.

The first main object of attention, apart from breast and bottle, is the mother's face. Brian, at one month, can exchange a look with his mother that lasts for some time. It has taken him a while to achieve this, although his mother has been able to enjoy the gradual build-up towards it of shared glances. It is a rather solemn look she gets, because Brian is not smiling as yet. But it is very rewarding none the less. Establishing this eye-to-eye link has been described by some who have attempted to research 'pre-verbal communication' as the first step towards speech itself.

There is a quiet rhythm to a baby's life in his early days which has the effect of imposing little strain on his strength and abilities. He sleeps, wakes, feeds, looks about him for a bit, then falls drowsy and has another sleep. During his waking time he may need to concentrate on what is going on inside him, by way of digestion or elimination. Most of this is quite outside his control, but it makes demands on his attention, none the less. Very gradually, if the rhythm is not greatly interfered with by his parents, he will spend less of his time sleeping or looking as if he will fall asleep any moment. His exploration time goes up—proportional to the advances he has made.

Some writers have described this rhythm as 'vegetative'. It seems like a cycle of events surrendered to passively by the baby, which is calculated to make him grow—much as if he were a vegetable. They separate out those features of a small baby's activity (little kicks, making noises, etc.) which are 'conative'. This word implies positive work on the baby's part.

At first he has little conative drive. But then it grows geometrically. Sometimes a baby's efforts will be directed towards one object that intrigues him, and by the time he comes to consider anything else he has lost most of his drive. This means that he may be exercising one set of muscles, and understanding one kind of object or activity, more of the time. This is part of the explanation of why babies develop at different rates, in different respects. (The other sides to this question are inherited personality and skill, and varying levels of maturity of brain and muscle.)

At this stage of life there is no point in trying to make him stop doing too much of one thing, or in trying to give him special exercise. If he seems particularly backwards in some way, this must be discussed with a doctor. But by and large, most babies even up in their achievements over time. To be 'late' in at least one thing is perfectly normal.

It is curious to consider that while your baby is warmly clothed, but lying down with his arms and legs unrestricted, kicking away and grasping at rattles, watches, and hair, other infants are tightly swaddled. This practice, whereby the baby is wrapped up into a kind of cocoon, was very common in Europe even in the nineteenth century. Now it is restricted by and large to parts of Russia, Eskimos, Red Indians, and to a number of primitive tribes. Research has shown that when swaddled children are released from their bondage—at about 18 months—they are much less handicapped in finding their balance and learning ability than would be expected. In fact, they find their feet quickly, and within a month or so they are as well developed in walking as their western counterparts. This seems to point to *maturation* of the nervous system being more important than *exercise*. Were the babies to be un-swaddled when they were past the normal age of learning to walk, the effect might be very seriously different.

There are times within which a baby can make rapid progress at mastering certain kinds of things—whether they be activities or accomplishments that involve understanding. This is sometimes called a 'sensitive period', meaning the time when the child is particularly sensitive to cues that help him to learn something. When this time passes it may be much more difficult for learning to take place, and the child may remain backward, or he may miss a stage.

There is a school of thought that holds that the first month is the time when learning is in fact at its *fastest*: that the difference between a child of one day and thirty days, in terms of all kinds of development, is greater than over any other 30-day period. This may be so, and the rate of learning (when this is considered across *all* fronts) may gradually decrease from then on through life. But much of the first month's progress is low-key, and a mother who is very much absorbed in making sure that everything is all right in food intake and growth rate may not perceive all the things that her baby is doing.

From a mental point of view, the big experience in the first month must be his gradual discovery of his mother—as a person, who has a face that smiles, and a voice that soothes. She is not just a convenient source of milk or a changer of nappies. When they exchange looks at the end of the month there is an awareness of a person, and the protective half of a two-person team. This kind of feeling will grow, and any threat to this arrangement in the first five years is well known to be very serious in its consequences for personality, confidence, and the ability to build close relationships. But its basis is laid *now*.

Chapter three

Early feeding, and the mother-child relationship

No two babies are alike when they are feeding, whether at the breast or at the bottle. Some will gulp impatiently, and tend to make themselves sick. Others will approach their source of nourishment more calmly, and contemplate their mother while feeding, with a cool philosophic eye. The amount they want at any one session may remain remarkably constant, almost as if they were nutrition experts, or it may vary greatly.

The physical needs of these children at this point are more or less identical. What differs is their approach towards satisfying those needs. A lot of the personality of the child seems to be coming out in his approach, even at this early period. Of course, the differences in babies' feeding behaviour also reflect the mothers' skill, enjoyment, nervousness, and patience during the operation. Both a mother *and* her baby's inborn personality are contributing jointly, each to a greater or lesser extent according to the individuals, to the way he goes about it.

Here are two contrasting accounts, by mothers whose babies were both firstborn children, and were both a month old, within a few days of each other.

> When I had Timothy I firmly believed that I had to breast-feed him. In hospital, they regarded me as a bit of a nuisance, but were content to let me try. I was utterly exhausted when he was given to me for the first feed, and it was hopeless trying to make contact with each other. So I settled for the bottle. I regret it a bit, I suppose, but Timothy seems to be doing all right. He's entirely unpredictable from one day to the next. I'm never sure how much feed I have to get out of the fridge and warm up. Sometimes he takes an ounce or so in a great rush, as if his life depended on it.

Then he'll turn his head away, stare at the ceiling, and take no further part. (Even when he's had a good burp.) Then another time he'll be sort of slow-and-steady-wins-the-race, and then I know he's getting what he should. I used to worry about the fact that he often had much less milk than the clinic chart said he should get. But the health officer said not to worry, and whenever they've weighed him he seems to be doing OK. Just recently he went through the night twice running—from half past 10 to about 6—and my husband and I said whoopee, here we are. But Timothy's not like that. He's woken me up between 3 and 4 ever since.

Timothy added to his mother's anxieties by vomiting, on occasion, most of his feed. But despite his refusal to follow an even course, his mother was able to draw comfort from his physical progress. Although she felt he was puzzling, she *enjoyed*, as well as loved her baby.

I've really had no trouble with Anthony at all. I was able to feed him straight away, almost, except that they gave him some supplementary stuff from a bottle for the first day or so. He seemed to know exactly what to do, and how to do it. All I did was just provide. I thought he should be fed whenever he wanted it, but he very soon chose to ask for it every four hours. He was almost like clockwork, really.
Last week I started keeping on with him a bit longer at the 10 o'clock feed. He's slept for longer, but he doesn't *quite* go as far as 6 o'clock yet. But I feel we'll be free of the 2 o'clock feed before long. Quite honestly I've never worried about his weight for a moment. He gets his food, and he's obviously been putting it on. They've always seemed perfectly satisfied with him at the clinic.

Two completely different histories—and two very similar results, from a physical point of view.

Table 2 shows how babies generally gain in weight over the first few months. The two numbers in brackets under each average show the range that includes *most* babies, at each stage. In fact, a number of babies stray either side of this wave band from time to time. Premature babies are an important example. A bout of colic, some disturbed feeds, a minor, passing ailment can all contribute to a temporary halt in progress. In most cases,

22 Early feeding, and the mother-child relationship

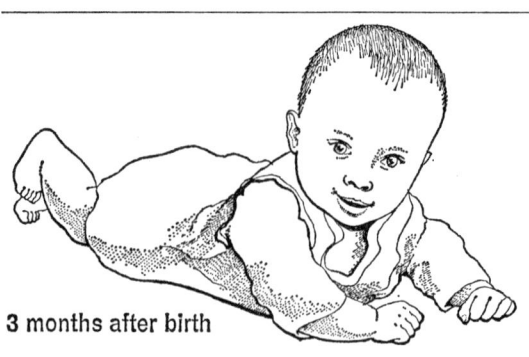

3 months after birth

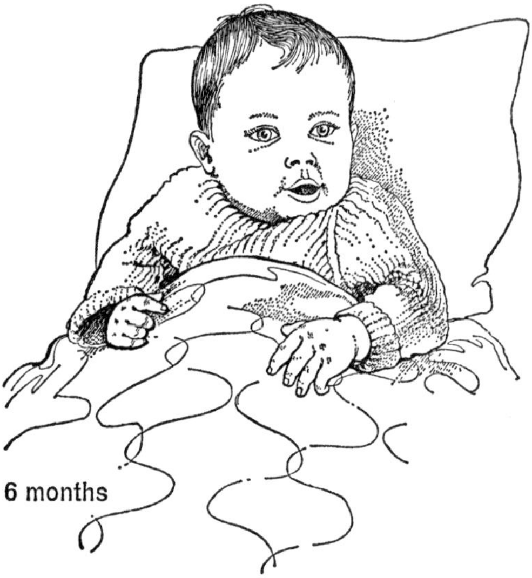

6 months

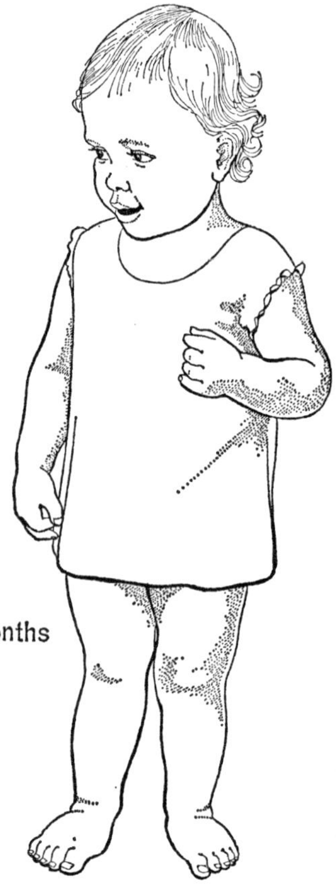

18 months

Diagram 1 Stages of growth

Early feeding, and the mother-child relationship

2½ years

Table 2 Babies' growth: weight and height

	Average weight	**Average height**
Birth	7½ lbs (5 to 12)	21 in. (16½ to 25)
3rd day	7 lbs (4½ to 11)	20½ in. (16 to 25)
1 month	8½ lbs (6 to 13)	22 in. (16½ to 26)
2 months	10¼ lbs (7¾ to 14½)	23½ in. (18 to 27½)
3 months	12 lbs (9½ to 16½)	25 in. (20 to 28½)
6 months	17 lbs (14 to 21)	27 in. (22 to 30)
1 year	21 lbs (19 to 25)	30 in. (25 to 33)
2 years	26½ lbs (22½ to 30½)	34 in. (30 to 37)
3 years	31 lbs (26½ to 35)	37 in. (33 to 41)

Notes
1 The first figure, against each age, is the *average* for girls and boys together. Girls are usually slightly lighter than boys, and very slightly shorter.
2 The figures in brackets show the *range* within which the great majority of babies are expected to fit. Young premature babies may weigh as little as 3½ lbs at birth.
3 To assess likely adult height:
Boys: Double the height at 2 years and add 2 inches;
Girls: Double the height at 2 years and subtract 2 inches.

this does not last long. A prolonged halt and no apparent interest in food is serious and must be referred to a doctor. The same applies to any *loss* of weight; or to continued increase in weight that is *greater* than that shown on the diagram.

How much food should a baby receive, in order to grow bigger in a normal way? As a rough guide, an intake of one ounce to every 2½ ounces of the baby's weight at each feed, is regarded as the norm. But babies are impatient with norms. At different times in paediatrics, some authorities have favoured the bottle over the breast on the grounds that it makes it possible to deal in strictly measured quantities. Women vary in the amount of milk they produce, and in the first few hours after birth, the speed with which they change from having a small volume of rich colostrum to an abundance of milk. This much is true: but most women are perfectly capable, physically, of producing ample milk for their baby. The main exceptions will be when the mother is ill, or when she has had a multiple birth. Both with breast- and with bottle-feeding, a mother is likely to worry more than is necessary, that her baby is getting the right amount. This applies particularly to babies who tend to build up wind too rapidly to continue feeding in comfort; to those who bring back a proportion of their feed; and to those who unaccountably nod off to sleep soon after starting.

Mothers would probably worry much less if they realized that feeding is rather like sleep. A baby feeds deep, in the first minutes of a feed. Thereafter, he usually takes things more easily, when the basic biological need is satisfied. Sleep is at its deepest, usually, early on in the night.

Diagram 2 shows how milk supply develops for most mothers who breast-feed. The example it represents assumes that a mother starts breast-feeding soon after giving birth, and continues until three months have elapsed. She then goes on to bottle-feeding, and the supply gradually dies out, without help of drugs

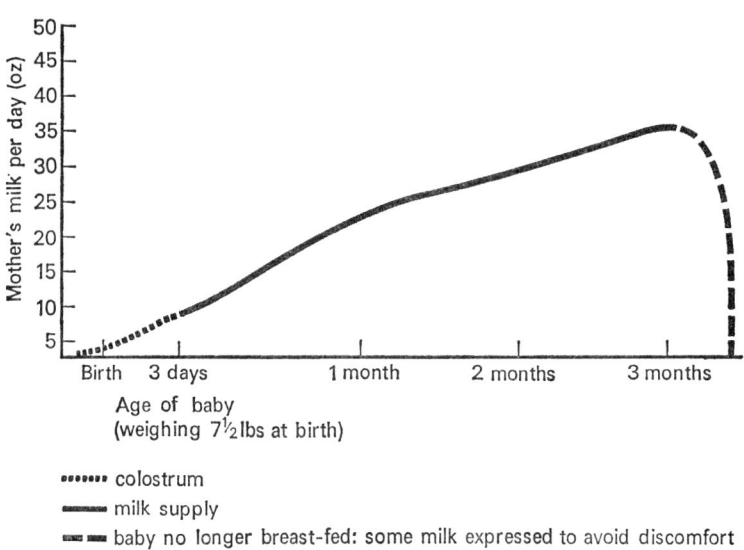

•••••• colostrum
▬▬ milk supply
▬ ▬ baby no longer breast-fed: some milk expressed to avoid discomfort

Diagram 2 Breast feeding: typical pattern of supply

of any kind. The solid line shows the average number of ounces she is likely to provide in a given day, if her health is good, and if she does not break the sequence. The baby's demand is a big factor in milk supply. In fact, there is nothing to stop a mother who is breast-feeding happily, from continuing for a month or two, or even more.

Obviously, some mothers continue breast-feeding long after three months. By then, other food is usually being taken, so that the amount of milk available from the mother is not crucial to her baby's progress. Her supply may in fact continue to arrive in good quantities right up to about nine months, although it will usually decline. Several factors enter in here. First, some women are physiologically better equipped for long lactation; their hormone balance may favour it more; and, which is at least as important, they may continue breast-feeding more *regularly* than others. (When a baby moves on to solids, and is producing more, sharper teeth, his mother may reduce the number of times she offers her breast—if only for self-protection. This reduces lactation.)

Table 3 Feeding

Birth	Breast-feeding or bottle-feeding. (Change to bottle possible.)
	5 feeds per day (average range is 3–6).
3rd month	Introduce a little cereal, and/or veg., meat, fruit *purée*.
	4 feeds per day.
5th month	Wean off breast/bottle, introducing milk in beaker.
6th month	Weaning likely to be complete.
	Baby may begin to feed himself.
	Introduce biteable foods—rusks, etc.
1 year	Drinks by himself.
	Introduce more 'family' foods (what the others are eating).
18 months	Independent in feeding (but needs help when tired).

Starting to eat cereals, rusks and other solid food usually happens in a baby's second or third month. Clinics and doctors recommend that the introduction should be gradual. If there is resistance to cereal on the first two occasions, it is often wisest to drop it for about a week, and introduce it, gently, at a different feed. This has two advantages: the baby does not feel under pressure (which could put him off cereal and disturb his feelings towards mother) and his mother is in an easier, less anxious mood, which can itself upset her baby's feeding.

Table 3 shows the kind of balance between milk and solid food, of different kinds, that most babies would be expected to be taking, at different ages. It must be stressed that some babies will be slower, some faster, at taking to different foods, and that provided they are gaining weight reasonably, and receiving protein and vitamins, they will be none the worse for it. Further, many children completely reject one food or other. There is a theory that, many times, they may be right. That is, they may have a slight allergy to what they avoid, or have comparative difficulty in digesting it properly. This cannot be tested and proven, for obvious reasons, but it is not wildly improbable, given that very young children have been shown to be able to balance their diet naturally, in a 'cafeteria-choice' situation.

Breast-feeding has a particular role to play from a physical point of view. For a normal baby, it is by no means a crucial role, but it means that in the first week or so following birth, there is more protection against a range of illnesses. These include colds, throat infections and gastric trouble.

The principle is that a mother's own immunization is passed on to her baby via her milk. This is desirable in all babies, but it is particularly important for premature babies. Since these have very little resistance to a germ or virus, and since they are too delicate for anyone to want to put at risk, most hospitals arrange for supplies of breast milk to be available in a bottle, should a mother not be able to feed her premature baby immediately, or at all.

But bottle-fed babies thrive, too. This prompts a parent to consider whether differences in feeding actually *matter*. A possible attitude to take is this: if most babies are going to end up, somehow or other, within a fairly wide range of 'acceptable' weight, whether they are quick or slow at taking to breast or bottle, and at becoming weaned successfully, does it really matter how they feed? Should a mother worry about doing things in a particular way, rather than just muddling through, waiting for problems to sort themselves out, and making sure that she and her husband are not unduly inconvenienced?

There are separate issues involved. Firstly, if there is a serious suggestion that a baby's growth rate is abnormal, and if feeding presents unusual difficulties, then concern for health comes first. Advice from the local clinic doctor or your g.p. should be sought. The fact that there *are* exceptions, that some babies do have abnormal problems that require abnormal solutions, means that the precaution of seeking medical advice *has* to be taken.

But the second point is that most problems are transient. This means that when the nurse or the doctor implies that the problem you are presenting them with has been seen many, many times, and has been successfully dealt with as often as that—this should be accepted as reassurance. Statistics show that babies choose many routes to the same end. There is an implication here, therefore, that peculiarities in feeding, and difficulties of understanding between mother and baby at feeding times should not be reasons for alarm from a *health* point of view.

Quite separate from this, however, are the questions of the development of the baby as an individual; and of the growth of communication between mother and baby. Put bluntly, feeding problems may have more of an effect on the psychological, than on the physical development of the child.

The first dialogue, perhaps, to be established and expanded over time between a mother and her baby is communication about feeding. Whether her baby is breast- or bottle-fed, a mother has to introduce him to his source of food, and to try to see that the circumstances are right for feeding, from the baby's point of view. Sometimes she will understand what he seems to be wanting, or objecting to: whether he feeds better in a particular position, with no one else around, and so forth. At other times, she will misunderstand him: she may think he has had enough when he turns his head and seems to lose interest, but miss the point that he wants to take everything more slowly that day, and just feel her for a while. Normally, misunderstandings decrease over time, although most babies contrive a surprise or two when least expected. But the whole process is one of repeated dialogue, in which many variations of relationship are explored. It is the first of these (if holding and cuddling are excluded) which involves a co-operative job between the two. Both are learning to achieve something better, by understanding each other better. This is why psychologists have sometimes considered that what happens in feeding lays the basis for all important relationships within the family, and for the whole personality structure of the baby himself.

Possibly this is over-stating the case. But there are many experts who do not think so. They include in particular doctors and psychologists who have been impressed by the evidence from psychotherapy that the roots of mental disturbance are to be found in very early difficulties of relationship between mother and baby. But these are not exclusively followers of Freud, or of his followers and rivals. Psychologists who have tried to analyse animal and human activity that could be called instinctive, or hereditary, have been forced to examine early feeding behaviour very carefully: their concern has been to differentiate between behaviour variants that a child would develop anyway, and others which are individual and determined by peculiarities of the mother-child relationship. They tend to conclude that a person's expectations from other people and his ability to communicate with them is very much influenced by early feeding.

Of course, it is one thing to say that this is likely to have a big influence over one's character, but it is quite another to assume that all will be ruined if things go wrong during this period. There are, after all, many other ways in which a mother gets close, tends, and expresses love to her baby. These must and do provide compensations in those situations where feeding seems to be a series of misunderstandings.

The communication aspect of early feeding has implications for whether feeds should be supplied at regular intervals, or on demand. Starting with set times (usually a feed every four hours), seems more reassuring in that it guarantees an even series of feeds that could not possibly leave the child under-nourished. But in practice, if feeding is on demand, few babies will often go beyond four hours before asking for a feed—although most of them will go beyond this period *sometimes*. The net result is very much the same, in intake and in weight gain. What are not the same, are the questions of the convenience to the mother, and the kind of communication that is established between mother and baby. An inexperienced mother may at first misinterpret *all* crying as a demand for food so that she supplies many short feeds, at infuriatingly short intervals. Eventually, she gets to understand his other needs, and when he is likely to give voice to them.

Feeding on demand means a two-way communication pattern from the start. A baby soon realizes that the procedure depends partly on him, and what he does. Since few mothers would be so rigid as to stick to the minute when a feed is due before giving in to a wail for food, the baby who is fed at set times is not wholly without experience of getting something at his request. It is more a question of degree.

The same judgment might be made about the case for breast-feeding, as opposed to bottle-feeding.

It is worth considering in some detail the kind of interaction that takes place, when the baby is being breast-fed.

The baby	The mother
Feels hunger pangs, and cries. (Or is roused.)	Hears her baby: recognizes it is time.
Notices: shapes suggestive of a feed coming soon; sounds that are associated with it; felt sensations that are associated with it; and the smell of his mother and her milk.	Feels the state of her breasts (full, possibly uncomfortable, sore, etc.).
	Prepares the situation for the feed—this includes going to a special room, making herself and baby comfortable, etc.
Learns how to take the breast; and how to anticipate this by holding and guiding it.	Offers her breast to baby—in whatever way she finds works best.
Sucks—gets better at it.	
Notices different kinds of pressure corresponding to the state and time of the feeding sequence.	Notices variations in baby's responses: she waits, or coaxes, encourages or discourages, helps.
Associates the same person who looks at him, talks to him, cleans and makes him comfortable, with the source of food. (In fact, she *is* food.)	Experiences pleasure (and possibly some discomfort): at least partially communicates her feelings to the baby.
Gets more efficient at sucking.	Exchanges looks with baby; perhaps talks, sings.
Plays with the breast—manually and orally.	Makes judgments as to whether the baby is replete, or still hungry, about to go to sleep, to have wind, pains, etc.
Exchanges looks with mother.	
Is aware of satisfying or painful feelings in his stomach, and reacts to them.	Copes with wind, performs a ritual closure to the feed.

These lists can be taken as a minimum. Clearly, a lot is going on. For the job to go well, both have to work up a competent understanding, and recognize little signals from each other. It can be regarded as a basic practice ground for trial and error in getting to know the other party. Both the seriousness and the pleasure to be gained from the job for both of them make it probable that the lessons received on this practice ground will be important enough to remember, and to build on.

Bottle-feeding is obviously not the same. A glance at the lists shows that once 'bottle' is substituted for 'breast', much, but not all of the points involving intimate communication simply vanishes. Yet it must provide important opportunities for forming the attitudes mother and baby will have towards each other, and for influencing the way the baby approaches the world. Breast-feeding is a personal event. This is no reason why bottle-feeding should be treated impersonally. Although it allows for others to help a mother out, and release her for other interests, authorities agree that a baby benefits from being bottle-fed by a single main supplier—preferably the mother. This is more likely to establish early on the desirability of satisfactory deep relationships with other people, in getting them associated with a primary benefit like feeding: the alternative is to encourage the child to assume that more casual relationships are adequate. In a household where anyone might be the next to feed, hold, cuddle, bath, or change the baby, his relationships must be more casual, less deep. This must be expected to persist through his life: partly because his earliest experiences of getting primary needs satisfied do not allow anything deeper, and partly (it must be admitted) because a household where life for a baby begins this way, will not change.

Feeding is central to early care. Mothers who cannot breast-feed—including those who wisely decide that the problems they have met trying to breast-feed make it unwise to force the issue—will normally feel like compensating for the loss of contact that using a bottle means. There is plenty that can be done to make the experience close, and not casual. First, by setting the scene as a private event. This includes making it for mother and baby alone, in quiet. An onlooker should not be allowed to distract or interrupt the flow of dialogue, unspoken as well as spoken. Second, by considering the nature of understanding in terms of infant time, as opposed to adult time. Children often repeat questions, sometimes infuriatingly, so that they can gradually digest the same answers, and fit this information into their world. Babies are the same, at a more primitive level of thought. They need time in order to appreciate the niceties of feeding. This is a wholly different question from being able to receive a physically adequate feed. Associations between a kind of nudge, a kind of look, a way of being held, and different stages in feeding can only be formed into ideas by repetition and by being pondered by a baby who is not being hurried. Again, this is also a matter of degree: no mother has all the time in the world, on every feeding occasion. But a slow pace allows the advantages of contact, as well as making feeding problems less likely. Third, the mother using a bottle will often allow and encourage her baby to explore her own body. (This is more frequent, according to some authorities, among mothers who particularly regret not breast-feeding, or giving up breast-feeding.) Clearly, this fondling, which is a means of discovering, and repeating what one discovers about the mother, ties in the first feelings for the mother with the pleasure of being fed.

Compensation of this kind makes it understandable that while there is some evidence (see Chapter 5) that certain types of personality are associated with early feeding experience, it is comparatively limited. The evidence exists, but it is observed in clinical studies rather than the kind that is under strict scientific control. By contrast, there are statistical data on differences in personality between children of mothers who have rejected them, —i.e. where *no* compensations apply—and the average of other children.

Feeding does not stop when the food has gone successfully into the baby. For his own comfort, as well as for his mother's peace of mind, it is worth considering what happens to this food, so that the whole process is thought of as a single operation. This helps you to understand why your baby may suddenly stop concentrating on his food and attend to what is going on inside him. It should also suggest why a feed should not be hurried, either during *or* after the last drop has disappeared inside him.

Provided it is not gulped, so that some of it is vomited, food goes fairly quickly through the oesophagus into the stomach. This is a bag that is capable of great expansion. Food accumulates here until it has been processed into a suitable state for its journey through the intestines.

The problem, from a baby's point of view, is that it is not simply food that he takes into his stomach. Quantities of air find their way inside too. However elastic the sides of the stomach are, there is a stage when air has to be released before the baby can feel comfortable again, and before he can reasonably be asked to eat or drink more.

There is always *some* air in the stomach. When a baby is very small, his stomach is less used to changing shape, so it needs to reject some air. Alternatively, if a baby of any size is over-excited, or nervous, the stomach will not expand as easily as it might. The result, a need to belch, is the same.

Babies vary a great deal in their ability to get rid of wind easily. But some factors make it more difficult for them. Being hurried is one. Being fed from a bottle with a teat that has too small a hole is another. In both cases, a bigger ratio of air to food is going to be accepted. These factors are under a mother's control. What she cannot control, of course, is the speed with which her particular baby may launch himself at breast or bottle. There is an argument that demand feeding makes a child less anxious to get started than going by the clock, but there are personality differences here too.

A mother in a hurry, particularly if there are other children about, may find it impossible not to be impatient with a baby who seems to be feeling discomfort, but obstinately refuses to bring up wind. This is most likely to happen in the first few weeks, but it can be later too. The most sensible question is to ask: 'Does he *really need* to bring up wind?' By no means all babies do, and getting impatient with them is obviously pointless. Many babies have a characteristic look when they need to get rid of wind: it is a rather moody, preoccupied expression, and sometimes their lips purse and seem to be tinged with blue. A mother without the experience to recognize this in her own baby would do well to try to take the feed at a slower pace, and to try some quiet, gentle, and unhurried winding at intervals.

If breast-feeding, this can be between each breast, or if using a bottle, this can be after, say, 2-3 ounces, or when her baby seems to have reached what he regards as a 'natural break'. (The same can be done at the end, when her baby has finished sucking.) But if nothing happens at the early break, and the baby is happy to continue, there is no reason why winding should be protracted unnecessarily. More harm is caused by transmitting anxiety from mother to baby about a belch that never happens than by leaving excess air inside.

Holding a baby upright when winding is commonsense. There is no value in encouraging him to bring up his feed as well. Holding him close to her body, as opposed to turning him onto his stomach on a table, means that his mother is reassuring him, and emphasizing that closeness does not stop after he has taken food from her.

Very small babies often look startled when they produce a sudden belch. They are, genuinely, startled. This is why reassurance is important. Gradually, some babies come to understand that a belch helps them, and is a natural stage in the feeding cycle. Some motivation for them may be that they are producing what their mothers seem to want. But this is something over which they only ever achieve marginal control. If they sense that they are being pressured to conform, they are *more* likely to need to bring up wind—because their nervousness prevents their stomachs from expanding naturally—and they are *less* likely to achieve it.

If a mother and her baby achieve a kind of quiet communication over wind, to the effect that it is unimportant, but if it comes, then mother can *help*, then the bond between the two of them is made that much closer. For the baby, it is another association of his mother with physical well being. But if he is led to worry about what is happening inside him, about why wind is not coming on demand, and if it is a source of anxiety to his mother, that he feels but cannot understand, the association is between feeding and a kind of failure. Some have suggested that digestive and feeding problems that extend into childhood may have roots in anxiety fostered at this stage in life. It seems plausible, but it is virtually impossible to prove.

The difference between wind and 'colic' is disputed ground. 'Colic' is not so much an illness as a way of explaining crying as for pain, as opposed to annoyance. It may occur at any time from two weeks to three months (despite its common description 'three months' colic). A baby who signals distress, despite winding, attention, rocking, soothing, and so forth, should be referred to a doctor, who may prescribe a remedy, and give special feeding advice. Colic does not seem to be highly correlated with long-term after-effects for the baby. It is something of a medical mystery, but the trend is to doubt its existence.

After food travels through twelve feet or so of intestines, the waste parts of it, that the body does not require, arrive at the rectum. It is propelled along by a series of contractions, and takes three to four hours to reach its goal. These contractions do not take place at a uniform rate. When the intestines become more sensitive, whether because of the nature of the food or because the baby has a fever, or is simply excited, the contractions become more rapid. Even having a feed can produce this side-effect. The result of this is that a mother is sometimes left with the impression that her baby's feed has gone straight through his body. Doctors are often given this report, by mothers who believe that their children might therefore be ill.

Although it makes sense to check that a baby is comfortable before his feed, by seeing that he is not irritated by a wet or dirty nappy, it must be agreed that a clean nappy may need changing again soon afterwards. It is no good blaming the food, much less your baby, who has no control whatever over the event in his first weeks.

During this period, there are no fixed rules for the number or the nature of the bowel movements that a baby may have. These may be one, two, or six in twenty-four hours. They may be solid or liquid, and any shade of brown. What *is* worth noting, however, is a sudden change in the direction of constipation or diarrhoea. A change from three soft to one hard movement, say, particularly when there is also some obvious straining or stress in passing a movement, suggests constipation. A change from three soft to eight liquid, particularly if they are greenish, and smell very nasty, suggests diarrhoea. As a rule, constipation needs a mild corrective —a little boiled water containing some sugar is often recommended —and needs to be referred to a doctor only if it endures for several days. But diarrhoea can be more serious. Provided it is not obviously connected with the baby's first encounter with strained fruit (when diarrhoea is often an immediate but short-term reaction), a doctor should be told. It may be an early indication of an illness that needs treatment.

There is some difference, usually, between breast- and bottle-fed babies. Breast-feeding tends to influence softer, more frequent movements, with a less pungent smell. For these babies, the introduction of solids, or changeover to a bottle changes the character of the movements. This should not cause the mother any concern.

Waste matter cannot be felt, with any clarity, in the intestines.

In the rectum, however, its presence is evident. It is a pleasant experience, in a normal human being, to defecate. It gives pleasure all the more if the matter is felt collecting, and then expelled in a column. When this happens to a small baby, he has only a tenuous sense of participation in the event. But it gradually becomes more fun to build it up, and then get rid of it in one satisfying set of contractions. This is the start of control. It depends on pleasure. Either constipation or diarrhoea militate against this pleasure, for obvious reasons. The point has to be made that in the first weeks the timing of defecation is very much a personal, internal matter. What is natural for the baby is also *that which is calculated by nature to give him more pleasure, and therefore more control.* This is the basis for the argument against premature attempts at training.

A baby usually develops a particular expression which appears on his face when he is preparing to pass a movement. Mothers describe it variously as 'intent', 'determined', 'cautious'—choosing words that suit the interpretation that *they* put on the look. It may seem merely that he is concentrating on something special. Unless he is constipated, he will not look quite as discomfited as when he is suffering from wind: some babies, in fact, will positively beam. Recognizing this expression is the first really helpful step that a mother can take towards toilet training—or, rather, towards building an understanding with her baby which will lead to co-operation over this function.

The next step is to show your baby that you *approve* and are *pleased* with what he is doing. This does not mean smiling sweetly every time your schedule is ruined by an unexpected movement, or actually revelling in the task of cleaning up the more explosive messes. What is important is making your baby feel that he is doing the right thing. Disgust or impatience in a mother's face or tone can induce something akin to guilt, in terms of inadequacy to control something that is disturbing the feelings between him and his mother.

Some psychologists have suggested that passing a movement represents the first present that a baby can make. This implies more sophisticated mental images than seem likely in the first few months. But the act itself is certainly one of the first efforts where he can perceive a connection between what he does, or the state that he has reached, and positive action being taken by his mother. If it goes well, and if it is received well, this is another positive and pleasurable adjunct to attachment behaviour.

When a mother shows that she recognizes from the baby's face that he is preparing something of this kind, and is able to express encouragement, without disturbing him, and later to show approval when it is clear that he has passed his movement—then the association between digestion and communication becomes important, because it means co-operation and love. This signalling is the best possible start to training. Obviously it needs to be combined with a loving, and preferably a delicate touch when the baby is being 'mopped up'. This is very much part of his reward. What should we make of this mother's account?

When Jane was just over a month old, it was obvious that there were two feeds in particular after which I could expect to find she'd made a mess. I kept the pot handy at those times, and perched her on it towards the end of the feed. As often as not she produced something straight away. When she didn't, I held her to me, with the pot underneath her, and bounced her a bit in my arms. I reckon she got to know what I wanted pretty quickly. Of course, I got messes at other times, too, and I told her off for this in a mild way. When she was about three or four months old, I think practically everything was going into the pot. It saved a lot in nappy-cleaning time, and it meant a lot for my nerves. As soon as she could sit up without being held, she went on the pot twice a day, and she would come off as soon as she produced. Of course it didn't work every time. She's not quite perfect now [she is 18 months old] but she very rarely makes a mistake. When she does, she's very sorry about it.

Well, it worked, at the superficial level of saving Jane's mother some time and trouble. Her methods, however, are very likely to have affected Jane's personality, over a much longer period than these first few months. This is not saying that her life is ruined. The point is that her attitude towards those who are close to her, and her values, have been forced into a particular mould. The characteristics of those who have been subject to strict toilet training in early childhood are discussed in Chapter 5. A mother who shows that she sets a greater store by carefully collecting, isolating, and getting rid of waste matter than she does by building a close bond of love with her child, will encourage this type of attitude in her children. Being excessively house-proud—to the point where tidiness is venerated so much that the family are uncomfortable to be living there—is closely related to this. Formal toilet training in the first year, let alone the first four months, has little to be said for it.

Liquid waste matter is stored in the bladder, and expelled from the body through the urethra. The average time between ingestion of food and urination is shorter than in the case of solid waste. It is doubtful whether small babies are as aware of the process happening to them as they are of defecation.

The whole food cycle is far more than a matter of keeping a baby clean, growing, and comfortable. It offers, as this chapter has shown, a large number of opportunities for a mother and her baby to make and repeat close contact with each other; for communication between them to become established; for associations with his mother of all kinds of satisfaction, reassurance, and love to be observed and appreciated by the baby. The way he proceeds to relate to her over the following months depends very much on these preliminary experiences of her. A mother's aim throughout this period should be to allow no opportunity for her child to feel that some element in procedure (be it speed, or ritual, or in remaining clean) is in any way more important to her than he is himself. A baby likes ritual—if it is to his benefit, at his pace. But a baby who is not experimental is not exactly promising, and experimentation demands that those who are doing it feel flexible, and not under strict control.

The other main factors influencing success over this period are a mother's basic maternal feelings. Often these overcome all her previous fastidiousness over feeding procedures and dirty nappies. But sometimes they do not: she has then to make herself diagnose her feelings. Many do, with no little skill, and the result is a calmer, and better understanding with their babies. Lastly, there is the problem of time. No mother has enough time. But some make more time than others. A realistic time allowance for feeding allows for a possible doubling of the average feed time, in case the baby is troubled by tiredness or wind, and allows for winding and cleaning-up time too. If it can be stretched to take in fondling and exploration time, too, then the sheer statistical chances of mother and baby recognizing what each other is thinking and feeling are very considerably increased.

Chapter four
Up to six months

Describing the newborn child, it was mentioned that his arms and his arm movements were well in advance of his legs. This was only to be expected from the position, and the activity of his arms while in the womb. To some extent this continues right through life. The principle by which the part that is nearest the head gets developed first, and that which is nearer the end of the spine follows afterwards, is called 'cephalocaudal'. It is particularly easy to observe how this works during a baby's first six months.

To be able to control his body, and to do things with it, he first had to learn to shift his head. Getting to the point of holding his head steady, while his body is shifted, was the major achievement of his first month—even if he still could not hold it against gravity for long. To be able to do things like sitting up, standing up, and walking, he first has to get increasing mastery over the large object on his shoulders. As it is growing all the time, this is not the easiest problem. But his central nervous system is maturing in a way that allows the cephalocaudal principle to continue: that is, priority is given to getting the nerve connections right for controlling his neck muscles by conscious effort of the brain, before preparing for tasks involving the shoulders, the hands, the back muscles, or the legs.

It follows that a baby with more difficulty than others in moving his head is at a considerable disadvantage. In fact, there is some evidence that children with large heads are rather slower to sit up or to walk. But this is more a matter of the ratio, or the relationship between the size of the head and the rest of the body, than simply having a large head. Size of head can be hereditary, and so can the likelihood of appropriately sized muscular equipment, and so forth, for lifting and turning it. But children are not consistent in what they inherit. Therefore some 'big-heads' will take longer to be active. This will not necessarily mean that they are going to be less active as young children, once they are on their feet and running around. Time is quickly made up. But it *can* have a more subtle effect on their approach to getting things—if they become more used than others to having toys and attention brought to them, than to finding the quickest means of getting them for themselves.

It is worth pointing out here that fat babies do *not* seem, on average, to be any slower at moving about, and eventually walking, than thin babies. Illingworth is categorical about this: as consultant in the Children's Hospital at Sheffield, he has studied and compared many hundreds of children.

The first job to get right with one's head is how to hold it at the right angle to the shoulders and to the rest of the body that allows comfort and a good view around. After that, the progress is towards being able to lift the head up *above*, or *away from* the body line—to get an even better view, and to anticipate what comes next. The first job occupies the second month, and the business of pointing his head develops through the third and fourth months, in particular. It is not easy to draw a distinction between *keeping* his head steady, and *raising* it. He will only, in fact, be able to raise his head from 'favourable' positions at first—e.g. when lying on his stomach.

It should be remembered that his visual powers are increasing throughout the time that control over his neck muscles is being established. Improvement in the one is naturally encouraging to the other: the more you appreciate the use of your eyes, the more you try to use your head and neck to see different things. Similarly, the more you can adjust your body into a receptive position for seeing more things, the more incentive there must be to develop the ability to distinguish objects from each other, and to touch them if they move. Both these functions are partly a matter of muscle development, and partly a matter of the maturation of the brain and the rest of the central nervous system.

When we see a baby who is wide awake and looking with curiosity at the world, we often think of the word 'alert' to describe him. He looks as if he is ready to examine everything and anything. This aspect is very much dependent on his increasing command of what his head and his eyes can do.

Another function that is growing fast at this time, and which many parents ignore if they do not stop to think about it, is the ability to locate where a sound is coming from. Psychologists have been able to test this at successive ages, because babies will try to pay attention to a new sound if they can, provided it is distinctive enough and they are not engrossed in something like feeding. At three months, a baby will turn his head to whichever side a sound has come from. Before that, he could certainly hear —in fact, there is some research which suggests that even in the womb a baby hears and responds to a noise simulating his mother's heartbeat—but *placing* it is another matter. Research by Murphy has shown that between the age of three months and six months a baby first learns to distinguish sounds that come from a source to one side and below him; and then later he can tell if a sound is coming from one side and above him. Judging where a sound has come from when it is made at an equal distance from both ears (in any direction) is more difficult still. By the time he is a year old, the average baby can localize sounds about as well as he ever will. But the big sound searching period is from the third to the seventh month, which contributes greatly to the 'alert' look described above.

During this time he is also looking at toys and other objects in a rather hungry way, as if he would like to hold them and play with them. But they have to be handed to him, at least during his first four months. During his first two or three months, he still makes the grasp reflex, with which he was born (and which was described in Chapter 2). Gradually this is lost, and during his third month you can notice that his hands are now becoming clenched much less often, and are more likely to remain open when they brush against something.

At about three months he pats his hands together—rather clumsily—and explores the fingers of one hand with the other. He will pull at his clothes, if they are such as to let him get his hand under a hem. If he is given a plastic ring, he will hold it, and play with it for a while. At first it drops fairly quickly, after a few seconds. A sign that he is developing control over his hand movements is holding on to toys like the ring for longer and longer periods; and doing things with them, like hitting them with one hand, while still holding on to them with the other.

It is rather perplexing to watch a baby at this stage trying to grasp something for himself. Very often he aims—and misses. Sometimes he 'overshoots' and seems to push right through it.

On occasions he will go for it with both his hands outstretched, and somehow he may contrive to scramble it towards him. All this is not impatience, or anything wrong with his eyesight. His motor control, again partly muscle and partly brain, has to mature, and at the same time he needs to gain experience of what happens when he reaches for things in different ways.

By the end of his fourth month he should be able to pick a simple object up without too much trouble. He will still go for it with both hands, sometimes, but this often seems to be a matter of a baby's personal habit. He will then be making the acquaintance of his toes and his feet. Since he is almost bound to get more direct experience of these than of any other playthings, he quickly becomes proficient at grabbing them and handling them. They are an ideal 'educational' toy for the practice of eye-and-hand coordination.

As he gets better and better at this, his ability to retrieve objects he has dropped also improves. At six months, or sometimes a little later, there may be an interesting turning-point to watch for. In a baby's world a great deal happens as if by magic. A toy arrives, then disappears, and later arrives back again. The processes are not questioned. But as his visual powers improve, a baby notices where a toy he has been holding is dropping. At first he only seems to observe its progress if it has not got far to drop, and remains inside the range of his gaze. As his clutching powers improve, he begins to retrieve it too. Gradually he looks around for a toy that drops beyond his range. This is a puzzled, ineffectual search at first, but gets better with practice. Parents who do *not* always try to 'help' him by handing him back what he has momentarily lost, probably hasten his progress. Soon he is adjusting his own environment, instead of waiting for magic to do the job for him.

A baby who moves doggedly and consistently through these stages is showing signs of coping—albeit in a limited sense—with the events around him, and getting a basis for future self-sufficiency. But it must not be expected that every child will go evenly from one phase to the next, at equal intervals. He may slow down for a while, possibly concentrating on other interesting things. As his basic diet has changed—with all probability—during this time, his exploration of his surroundings may be limited to fingering cereal, and his spoon, and the beaker that appears one day at his lips. He has a lot of claims on his attention, not forgetting the new sights and sounds that he becomes more aware of as he is able to turn to look outside his pram. He may not lack curiosity simply because he is a bit slower than others at picking up and retrieving.

Skill at this *may* to some extent run in families. But a family that prides itself on it—e.g. 'my brothers were always clever with their fingers'—is more likely to encourage it in the next generation than others. The rate of myelination in the spinal column (one of the aspects of maturation of the central nervous system) does vary by heredity. This is fundamental to co-ordination. At the same time there is no evidence that babies who are not up to the average in their progress past early co-ordination milestones do not eventually become perfectly capable of complex manual skills, provided they are physically normal. On the other side, nobody should try to spot future virtuoso pianists among those who are more precocious at this age.

Two other physical developments in the six-month-old are very noticeable but less exciting than what has been so far described. These are hair, and teeth. After the first foetal hair is lost, soon after birth, some babies stay bald, while others replace it very quickly. By six months, most babies' heads will be very handsomely covered.

At the same time, most babies will have their first two teeth visible, or at least discernible as bumps in the gum. These are usually the two lower central incisors, to be followed shortly by two more lower incisors, one on either side. Nature has been rather unkind to human beings where teeth are concerned, and the baby's first experience of them is likely to be painful, as will later experiences. It is an opportunity for him to find comfort in his mother; even if she may feel that her rocking, singing, and even application of teething gel are somewhat ineffectual at times, all this attention is appreciated, and is a further step in their intimate relationship.

Toothache is, however, exaggerated by mothers who assume that a tooth must cause pain if it is emerging. Cross-cultural studies suggest we fuss too much.

44 Up to six months

Six-month-old ignores
toy which has fallen under the cot

Diagram 3 Eye and hand

Twelve-month-old looks
for toy under the cot

Up to six months 45

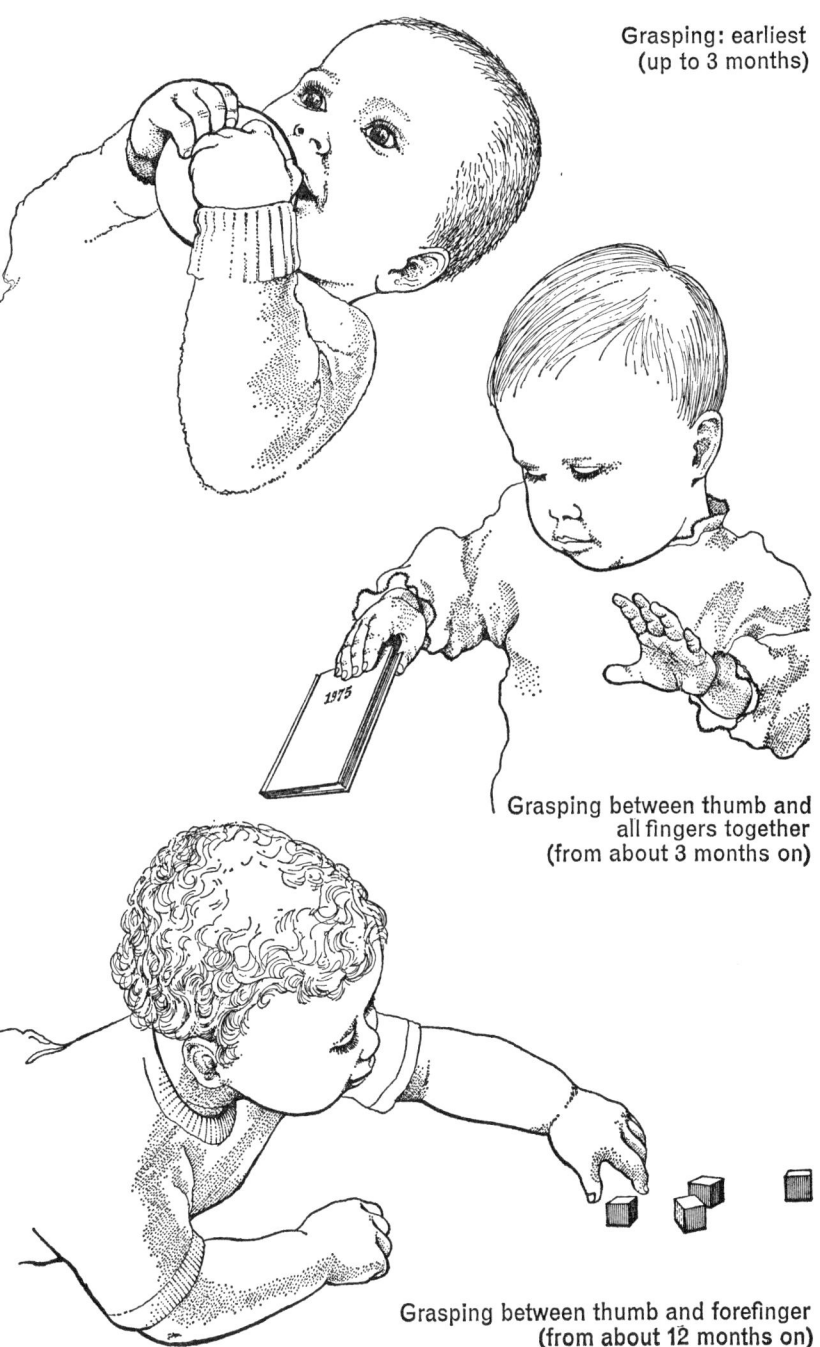

Grasping: earliest
(up to 3 months)

Grasping between thumb and
all fingers together
(from about 3 months on)

Grasping between thumb and forefinger
(from about 12 months on)

Some questions that parents ask during their babies' first year

1 He doesn't seem to be gaining much weight—what is wrong? Will it matter? Very few babies obey all the rules, all the time. There may be a week, or more, during which no weight progress seems to be made. He may even lose a little weight. When they do this, they usually make up for it soon afterwards. Several factors are often found to be responsible in some way for failure to gain weight. A mild infection, such as a cold; indigestion or colic; a shock of some kind—a fall, for example, sudden separation from mother, any other radical change in routine. What may not be a radical change for *you*, may be rather more serious for *him*.

If he seems all right in other respects—that is, if he is well, and a happy baby—then the only real problem is likely to be the mother's anxiety. But illness of any kind, and a weight standstill of more than one week in the first three months must be reported to the health visitor and/or the doctor. Loss of appetite suggests infection.

Naturally, the older a baby gets, the stronger are his reserves of strength, and the less a long weight standstill is likely to matter.

2 Can we tell at this stage whether he's going to be very intelligent or not? Not very accurately. Many children do not disclose their hand until a number of years have passed. Some attempts have been made to test large numbers of children at regular intervals. This has its uses—mainly as a diagnostic tool to check whether certain children need special help. But at the other end of the scale, results of tests of co-ordination, etc., do not seem to link up precisely with IQ results or success at school later. There *are* links, but they allow a lot of variations.

Some very exceptional children *do* seem to give advance notice (or warning!) of very high intelligence. This usually takes the form of a low sleep need, being early to exchange eye-to-eye looks, long, hard concentration on an object or a task, and of course early speech.

3 My baby seems to sleep much more than other babies. Sometimes he drops off before he's finished a feed. He seems perfectly well—but why should a baby be different in this way? How much sleep should my baby need? The only answer to the last question is 'as much as he wants'. Babies do vary a great deal over sleep. In the early weeks of life, those who sleep less often are usually asking for more feeds than others. Later, they seem to want more play-time or simply time spent with mother. There is no point in waking a sleeping baby up just to be part of the scene. A problem comes when a feeding schedule is upset because the baby sleeps past the time set for a feed. Some mothers wake him up then, to avoid having to go to sleep themselves and being woken an hour later. But this is best done only when the baby has been asleep for some time. If he continually disrupts the pattern, it may be the pattern that is wrong for him, and not the other way round.

Needing more sleep is a reflection of a central nervous system that has not matured. As the child gets older, need for sleep declines with the development of self-regulatory mechanisms in the brain. It seems likely that a baby who sleeps more than others has a more slowly maturing control system. Children who are precociously intelligent seem to need less sleep—and there is research evidence to back this. But a sleepy baby may also be one born with a more placid personality: it certainly does not follow that he is necessarily going to be less intelligent.

Some heavy day-time sleepers may be compensating for night-time disturbance. This can be for many reasons—a change in routine (e.g. weaning), fear of separation, or simply a need for more contact.

4 How does my baby actually suck? It is not just a question of placing the lips on either side of a nipple or teat and applying suction. The baby makes a sequence of movements. In breast-feeding, he first 'roots' for the nipple, and the stimulus of finding it in his mouth makes him apply pressure with his gums on the tissue around the nipple, forcing milk to flow into it. Then the sucking proper begins. Arguably it is the most complex set of reflexes the baby is born with. This makes it obvious why, for example, a depressed nipple is more difficult for a baby to get food from. In bottle-feeding, the baby tries the same principle, but adapts his work to the situation he finds—i.e. that the milk is continuously supplied to the end of the teat by gravity.

5 Sometimes it's very difficult to tell why he's crying. Why does he cry so much? Does he do it to exercise his lungs? Opinions on crying have changed over the past two or three decades.

Some questions

The advice that used to be given was that if a baby was well fed, winded, dry, and clean, but still cried—he should be left to cry away. He would come to no harm, and his mother had a right to some privacy.

Modern opinion, on balance, is that babies cry for a reason, and when they cry, something should be done about it. Their lungs get perfectly adequate exercise *without* long bouts of crying. Dr Hugh Jolly considers that, on the weight of psychological evidence in clinical studies, a baby cries a lot if he is bored or lonely, *or* if he is reflecting his mother's disquiet or unhappiness. Picking up a baby when he cries certainly does not 'spoil' him. Making someone happier is not tantamount to giving in to every whim. It also helps make *oneself* become less unhappy—although a mother who is under pressure cannot just be told to cheer up. She may need a sympathetic ear, and more help in the house.

A baby who suddenly takes to crying, despite a normally placid happy nature, *may* be in pain, and this should be discussed with a doctor.

Chapter five

Personality development

Apart from the excitement of seeing a healthy baby growing fatter and steadier, which is a particular pleasure during this period, there is the development of a distinct personality that is so fascinating. Some children, admittedly, seem to stamp their character on everything they do from Day One. But generally in the first month the time they spend asleep and the help they need all the time makes it difficult even for observant experienced parents to judge what special personality their baby may have. From the second month on, so much more of it unfolds.

A great deal of his personality is reflected in the looks that he shares with his mother. Often she will read into the way he looks at her all kinds of attitudes that would be much too advanced for this stage. But there is no doubt that mothers can sense at this time whether a baby is more inclined to be timid, or bold, or curious, or lackadaisical, or playful. There is all this variety, and more besides, in hereditary traits. There are many ways, too, in which these traits become encouraged, once a mother decides her baby is like that.

One characteristic that is hard to explain fully is how affectionate and loving a child seems to be. Mothers sometimes speak of their baby as being particularly cuddly; *or* particularly distant, or independent. Many psychologists, including those influenced by Melanie Klein, tend to feel there is a big inborn component in this trait. Others feel that since all babies have an instinctive attachment drive, it is how they have been treated that makes them seem more or less 'affectionate'. Certainly relations between mother and baby are very important for a child's future expression of love. It may be that it is the *degree* of their capacity to respond that varies on a hereditary basis, rather than a basic capacity as such.

Considering the question of the kind of personality traits that are much more likely to have been affected by early experience, rather than hereditary, Gabriel chooses these: the way a person reacts to affection, his capacity to give affection, and the way he asserts himself. Many other psychologists also tend to bracket together affection and confidence.

Where a mother is entirely bound up with her baby, thinks he is the most wonderful creature on earth, and loves and admires every little gesture he makes, the effect on the child's personality seems obvious. He enjoys the attention, the help, the kindness, the looks, and the cuddles that he gets: so he asks for more, and notices that he gives pleasure when he responds in particular loving ways, and imitates as best he can his mother's happy approaches.

That much is easy to understand. But what about the baby who is simply *not* cuddlesome? In a few cases, he may be handicapped —in a way that may delay his understanding of people, or using his eyes and his sense of touch to identify who is approaching him and how they are treating him. A baby with an eye problem, or an autistic baby with a disturbance of his perception mechanism, may be like this. They are very exceptional of course. A normal baby may have a mother who was not desperately keen to have him. Since this is not a feeling to which many mothers like to admit, she may 'project' her antagonism on to the baby: that is, she credits him with the unloving attitudes she is ashamed of, thus making it rather easier, as time goes on, to express a critical view of him— e.g. 'Well, he never liked me much, even as a baby'. This kind of attitude is quite unconscious, usually, and when confronted with the idea, a mother will naturally feel resentful. Another category of mothers are genuinely very loving towards their baby, but are extremely anxious about him, and about whether they are doing the right things. They can transmit their worries very clearly to the baby, who then shares their alarm as much as, or more than, their delight in their children's company. It is easy to see how this gets translated into 'not being a very cuddly baby'.

The capacity to give and share affection is certainly close to the centre of anyone's character. A very wide range of traits depend on it. Having confidence in others, being eager for their company, being interested in helping them, and wanting to establish deep and lasting relations with another person, are all reflections of it. Conversely, suspicion, envy, the desire to hurt or laugh at others, and all the problems of a natural reserve in committing oneself to a deep relationship—these are reflections of disturbed growth of this capacity. While there are a number of aspects of human nature that seem likely to have a genetic base, responding to love and expressing it seem to be very much matters of learning. Most of this important learning comes early in life, in the family.

Studies have been made of the difficulties that children and adults have in making friends, and in fitting in with society in general, when they have been separated from their mothers at an early age. The period up to five years appears from this work to be critical. Adopted children come off much better on a comparative basis—especially when adoption was *very* early—as against those who were forced to live in 'institutional' conditions. However kind the people are who run the institution, they cannot compensate a young child for loss of his mother except by providing a mother-substitute. This must be someone who *cares*, and who has a lot of time to devote to him.

A baby who has plenty of attention may yet fail to become entirely confident in his dealings with others if there is something threatening in the atmosphere—his mother's own insecurity may provide a threat, as may changes in her treatment of him or in the relations between the people around him. But whatever his mother is like temperamentally, a baby's main chance of self-reliance in the future is to be given a strong feeling that his mother is regularly close at hand and that even if she has to leave him from time to time, she returns regularly and predictably. She is the constellation in the sky by which he has to steer. (The name 'mother' should be extended to those who take on the role of mother-substitute, provided they fulfil it consistently and devotedly.)

This may seem to be over-stressing the mother's role in personality development—particularly to anyone who was himself separated from his mother, and is not conscious of anything wrong with himself. But the evidence—particularly the definitive work of John Bowlby on maternal deprivation and its effects—is very solid. Individuals protect themselves by forgetting childhood difficulties. When they discuss their childhood with, say, an uncle who observed objectively, some years afterwards, they are often surprised: 'of course, he was an *outsider*' they conclude. This is selective memory at work. Some very interesting experiments on monkeys brought up healthily but without the comfort or presence of their mothers show that when the time comes for them to pair off with their contemporaries, they are distinctly at a loss by comparison with those brought up normally. Arguments from ape to human are not always sound, but studies of children who are hospitalized, or brought up in institutions give strong suggestions that a similar principle is at work.

During the second month of a baby's life, adoption societies like to arrange the transfer of a child as quickly as possible. This is to prevent too close a relationship being formed between the baby and his natural mother, which could jeopardize the success of the changeover, and leave a scar.

It is in this second month that a mother receives a big reward for all her work. This, of course, is the first smile, which may be expected at about six weeks. At about the same time, or a little later, he will start making 'vocalizations' in her direction, possibly in response to her saying something to him (see Chapter 7 on Speech). The way that he continues smiling and producing sounds for people affords considerable clues about his personality and how he will express himself later (see Table 4).

Eysenck's work on personality led him to conclude that there were two main dimensions which explained most of the differences between people's personalities. The first dimension was being more extrovert, or more introvert, and the second was being more or less inclined to 'neuroticism'—that is, to worry, or to disturbance of one's intentions or mood. Glimmerings of both of these traits can be seen in very young babies. By about three months, many babies will be vocalizing a lot with other people who come up to the cot-side and say something to them.

They are typically extrovert, and have very little shyness or coyness at this age. They are usually positive towards ideas, too. That is, they will try to grab whatever seems to be offered to them —which many wearers of pearls will vouch for—and they will follow something or somebody with their eyes when he moves around the room. This means they are at the low end of this 'neuroticism' scale—at least for the moment.

But some babies are noticeably more withdrawn; others are noticeably more uncertain about what to watch or pursue, and are more distractable. These could be taken as signs of future personality—although this assumes that babies develop in a constant way, and observation shows that some change is always possible. Parents of gifted children—that is, those with high intelligence or a remarkable skill, sometimes comment that their child seemed to have the power to concentrate intensely, even in his first year.

Table 4 Social progress (up to 1 year)

Throughout first six months	Development of very strong attachment to mother, and constant need of her presence.
3 weeks	Looks closely at mother while feeding; then *shares* looks.
5 weeks	Smiles at mother (then at others too).
Up to 6 months	Responsive in open, friendly way to allcomers: smiles, vocalizes and laughs (3 months) spontaneously and in reply to overtures.
Throughout months 7–12	Continuing need for mother's presence; growing intolerance of her absence; but acceptance of regular pattern in her coming and going.
9 months	Has become discriminating when approached: greets familiars (especially father).
	Suspicious or shy (at first) with strangers.
	Responds to simple games—e.g. peep-bo, pat-a-cake, and tries to join in properly.
1 year	Needs a lot of attention: easily bored, frustrated and/or anxious if left for long.
	Increasing repertoire of games enjoyed with adults.
	Obeys easy instructions: likes 'getting it right'.

54 Personality development

Stretching hands out to mother

Shy of approaching adult (at 12 months)

Diagram 4 Social development

Personality development

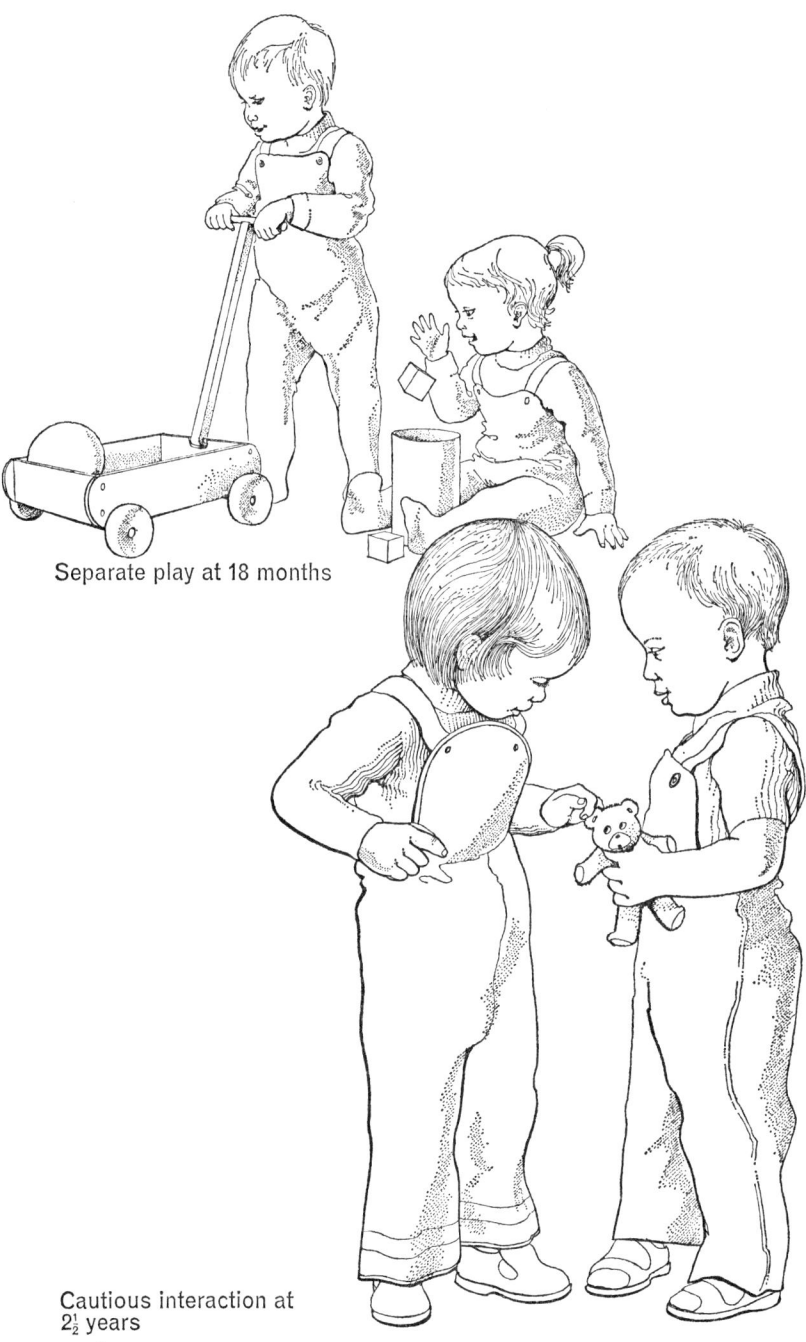

Separate play at 18 months

Cautious interaction at 2½ years

The development of curiosity in a child is very interesting. It could be said to lie at the root of many different aspects of character. Nothing could be easier than to discourage curiosity in a young baby: it only requires a belief that he should be fed, kept warm and clean, and then put firmly out of the way. It is by offering *time* that a child learns how interesting it is to explore. If you enjoy staying with him for a while after all the basic baby chores are through, and if you talk to him, put him within range of things he can grasp and play with, and if you encourage him like a companion (certainly not like a teacher) then you are helping him to be confident about examining the world and its people.

This does not demand a range of cunningly designed 'educattional' toys. (These are nice to give and to have, but not really necessary.) A baby needs his mother's time most of all, and her patience while she removes anything harmful from his approach, and allows him to finger his way through his cereal, yesterday's newspaper, a hairbrush, anything that strikes his fancy but does not involve *too* much clearing up afterwards. By the age of six months, most babies are very proficient at reaching for small objects and grasping them. He uses his whole fist to do it—not a very elegant movement as yet—and indeed he often uses both fists. But this essential skill for exploration builds up typically between the fourth and sixth month.

Two other progresses at this time are worth noting for their influence on personality. One is the gradual way in which the baby starts to treat his father in a particular manner. The detail varies greatly, but a notable feature is that father starts to be treated differently from mother. It often seems as if he is being regarded as the provider of fun, or at least a diversion from the constant interchange that is going on between himself and his mother—who is viewed as provider of food, of all basic needs, and of stability. Relations with father usually seem more relaxed, and less a matter of importance. Fathers arriving home in the evening often get, as a result, a cheerful grin, and a greeting which suggests they are just what was needed, which can be to mothers' annoyance.

This awareness of regular encounters with a familiar male face is considerably less important in giving a baby a sense of stability and confidence than the relationship with mothers. But it can modify personality very considerably: depending on how this goes, babies become more or less inclined to look beyond their mother;

and they may (or they may not) have the benefit of a less intense friendship that eases any strains which might be starting between baby and mother.

Father's influence seems less tangible than mother's. But he has a great deal to contribute, both by encouraging a baby to try out new things (that a mother may not think of, or have time to follow up), and by being a benign authority. He appears, he seems strong, he takes an interest, and he approves. His approval is prized—often more than mother's approval—and his disapproval can sometimes demoralize. Moreover his bond with the mother is seen as a source of strength and stability.

The second process is the development of a suspicion of strange faces. It is very difficult to know how this begins. Up to about six months a baby will smile or vocalize at anybody, as a rule. But in the sixth month, or a bit later, he starts discriminating. Some babies are particular: they show distinct preferences for men or for women with glasses, or for adults rather than children, etc., according to whim. Others become shy or fearful with anyone. The explanation is possibly the fact that they have begun to associate approach by a stranger with separation from the mother, even for a short time. This is plausible. The association would also be with diminished attention from the mother—which seems to make sense in cases where the baby treats a familiar friend of the family as if he were a stranger. But whatever the reason, the openness of the baby has changed into a situation where he may turn defensive. How a baby copes with his disquiet when a stranger is around reveals a lot about how his character is developing. Some babies are more fearful, some are more withdrawn and shy. Some can be teased out of it with heartiness, others have to be coaxed patiently, like alarmed cats. Some seem to go from fear to coyness very quickly, while others give you the feeling that they are consulting their dignity, before deciding whether there is common ground with the stranger. But all are happier if their mothers stay around. The *degree* to which mother's reassuring words actually soothe him says something about the general confidence she has given him—although, of course, this cannot be told from one particular meeting with one particular stranger on a particular day. All babies have their off-days.

So far not a word has been mentioned about the *psychosexual development* of a young child, or how this affects his subsequent personality. This is the territory of Freud, and his followers.

Many of his theories have been condemned for being unscientific, or for going far beyond the evidence he had before him. The point has also been made against him that his discoveries about human nature may be limited to abnormal people, suffering mental disturbance, and abnormal people in turn-of-the-century Vienna at that. But so much of his influence persists, and so many of his ideas have been supported by later workers, that a brief run-down of how a child develops in *his* terms is entirely justified.

The Freudian view of personality is that the major characteristics of an adult are directly derived from the very earliest experiences. Freudians are by no means alone in that. But to understand exactly how they believe that this happens, the principle of infantile sexuality must first be explained. Freud was struck by the evidence of repressed sexual desires and fears that he uncovered when he guided his patients through psychoanalysis back to their earliest childhood. The notion that sexual desires might be in children was abhorrent to those who first read what he propounded, but it does not really shock many people now.

Freud came to the conclusion that the basic motivating drive in a human being is that which becomes obvious as 'sexual' after puberty, when there is conscious interest in the reproductive work of the body. Prior to this, he believed, the driving force must always have been there—but concentrated on other 'erogenous zones'. When a baby is born, he goes through an 'oral phase', in which his energies are concentrated on the mouth, which is the source of all his pleasure. During the first months, rooting and sucking are the main ways of using his mouth. The fact that sucking is protracted, even when a baby is not actually feeding, was felt to be significant. When teeth start to appear, and he is encouraged to eat solid foods, progressing from soft to hard, the baby moves on to biting and chewing, which he finds pleasurable too. Sometimes he will revert to sucking: Freud noted that this was often done by young children in times of stress, or when they were behaving in several 'regressive' ways at once—e.g. crying and whining instead of talking. Gradually the mouth becomes less important, and at some stage usually in the third year the anus takes over as the centre of pleasurable attention. This 'anal phase', in turn, gives way to the 'phallic phase' sometimes in the fourth year. Attention is then more on the penis, in a boy, or on the clitoris in a girl. This is followed by the Oedipus Complex, and the Electra Complex respectively, after which there is a Latency

Period. Finally, with puberty, there is promotion to the 'genital phase' when individual genitals become regarded as part of a basic function, rather than as individual features with unusual potential for delight (see Table 5, p. 61).

Three main kinds of thing can happen to a child passing through each phase. He can be allowed satisfaction of the desires to use his mouth, or to explore parts of his body that interest him and please him. *Or*, he can be deprived of much of the pleasure that he is looking for—by early weaning, by inadequate or impersonal feeding, or by making him feel worried and guilty every time he touches what his mother feels is taboo. A third possibility is allowing and encouraging excessive gratification: some argue that this is different from satisfaction, from the child's point of view, because when his activity is *eventually* discouraged, it is all the more frustrating.

If a person is born with more sensitivity in certain parts of his body, this can affect their progress through these phases. In this way, then, Freud imagined that genetic factors played their part. But environmental factors—in particular, how a mother (and, to a lesser extent, father) treats the child in matters affecting the phase he is at—are of paramount importance. Frustration, *or* overindulgence, can lead a child to become 'fixated' on that phase. Explaining the concept of 'fixation' could take a few pages, but it will be enough here to say that it implies that the child attaches undue importance to that on which he 'fixates'.

The importance of this for personality formation is that fixation at a particular phase affects the child's outlook on life, on himself, and on his family. Other factors are involved, naturally, as the child grows up, and as further experiences incline him more to self-confidence or anxiety, to friendliness or hostility. Particularly important is the question of how a child's 'Oedipus Complex' is resolved, at about the age of six—which is outside the scope of this volume. But early fixation, according to Freud, throws a very long shadow.

There are certain traits called 'oral', others 'anal'. There are some 'phallic' ones, too, and some Freudians have even postulated some 'urinary' ones, but it is the oral and anal traits which are held to be the crucial ones for determining what a person is going to be like.

Complete satisfaction of early sucking desire, with unrestricted access to his mother's breast, and gradual, slow weaning while further sucking opportunities are provided (e.g. orange juice bottle, dummies, etc.) and the baby is left free to suck thumbs, blankets, or whatever he likes, can lead to an optimistic character, dependent on others, who expects the land before him to flow with milk and honey without much effort on his part. Frustration at this stage, however, can lead to a feeling that life has not so much to offer, that people are not to be trusted, and need to be pressed hard if they are to give affection or help.

Further details of oral types and anal types are given in Table 5. A great deal of research has gone into checking just how much of all this is myth, and how much is fact. For obvious reasons, it is extremely difficult to prove that people with particular personality types had particular weaning or toilet training experiences. Parents' memories of exactly how they brought up their children have been shown by the Newsons to be unreliable from about a year after key events. How much less reliable are children's memories? But some ingenious tests have been devised, which include cross-cultural comparisons between countries or races where conventions of infant care are known to be different in ways that should logically affect oral or anal fixation. The evidence has been summarized by Dr Paul Kline. There *are*, in fact, reasonable grounds for an objective conclusion that there is such a thing as an anal character, which may well have part of its origin in strict toilet training. The search for substantiation of oral characters and how they are formed has been less successful. But many Freudians will claim that the evidence is good, and that since the various parts of Freudian theory are interdependent, this too should be accepted.

There is little point here in trying to do more than introduce this aspect of child development in what seems the fairest way possible. If it all seems far-fetched, it is worth noting that many of Freud's ideas—for example, that people have unconscious ideas that influence them without their knowing it, or that unwelcome thoughts are often repressed from memory—are accepted now, whereas they seemed fanciful not long ago.

Freud's theories in this area have probably been the most influential, which is why they are given prominence here. In fairness, it should be added that others, notably Melanie Klein, have constructed their own diagrams of personality development, which also deserve attention.

Table 5 Some aspects of personality development according to Freudian theories of infantile sexuality

Pre-birth	Heredity and development in the womb affect personality by influencing the *sensitivity* of a child's body zones.	
Birth	Oral Phase Sexual pleasure is derived mainly from the mouth—through sucking...	Fixation leads to: Optimism and patience (through over-satisfaction). Pessimism and impatience (through frustration). Dependency, sociability, generosity.
6 months	Through biting and chewing.	Ambition, envy, jealousy, aggression.
2 years	Anal Phase Sexual attention is focused mainly on the anus.	Parsimony—meanness, hoarding, collecting, etc. Orderliness—sense of time, hatred of mess, bottling up emotions, etc. Obstinacy—insistence on individual view, resentment of pressure, etc.
4 years	Phallic Phase Sexual attention focused on: *Boys* *Girls* Penis Clitoris Castration Fear Castration Suspicion Oedipus Complex Electra Complex	Courage; rashness; self-importance.
6 years	Latency Period	
12 years	Genital Phase	

Chapter six

Moving around and walking: up to one year old

A large number of things happen when a baby is eight or nine months old. Sometimes a radical change seems to have happened overnight. This is when a baby who was for so long predictable and restricted in his movements, suddenly seems to turn into a danger both to himself and to all the family possessions. Instead of sitting quietly on the floor, he may pull himself up on a table leg, reach for the edge of the table cloth, and tug downwards. Instead of simply rolling over, so that instead of lying on his back he lies on his front, he may start to roll over and over, crossing the room much faster than was ever thought possible. Another baby will place both hands on the floor, one on either side of his bottom, and shuffle around. Parquet floors and tiles help this kind of progress, but again the speed developed is often remarkable. Finally, one week, a child may try ineffectually to move his limbs in a crawling fashion, but only contrives to move backwards, which brings a rather surprised look to his face. Not long afterwards, he may suddenly get the hang of using his knees to help propel him forward. The span of time it takes for him to learn to cover the room is then negligible (see Table 6).

Table 6 Learning to walk and run

Birth	Reflex action only. Much of this disappears as controlled movements are developed.
1 month	Can hold head (for a moment) in line with the rest of the body, when held up with a hand under his stomach.

Moving around and walking: up to one year old

2 months	Lifts chin off the bed when lying on stomach.
3 months	Lifts chin and shoulders off the bed—right up—and keeps them there for a few moments.
	Brought into sitting position, still lets head flop slightly.
4 months	Brought into sitting position, holds head steady, with back less rounded.
	Lying on his back, can 'kiss his toes'.
6 months	Can support his head and chest by leaning on his hands.
	When held upright, can take his weight on his legs.
	Sits in a high chair (supported, or 'locked in').
8 months	Rolls over: first from lying on back to lying on stomach.
	Crawling: first experience—usually backwards.
9 months	Crawls forwards, levering with his hands.
	Pulls himself up into a sitting position.
	Can stand if posted next to furniture, on which he holds himself up.
10 months	Crawls, using hands and knees.
1 year	Walks, held by both hands (later by one hand) or holding to furniture.
	Crawls, using hands and feet.
15 months	Stands up without help or holding you.
	Walks without help or holding on.
	Climbs stairs by crawling.
18 months	Walks with assurance (e.g. stops, turns, carries objects without overbalancing).
	Climbs stairs by walking (but often needing support).
	May start jumping.
2 years	Runs (not always safely).

64 Moving around and walking: up to one year old

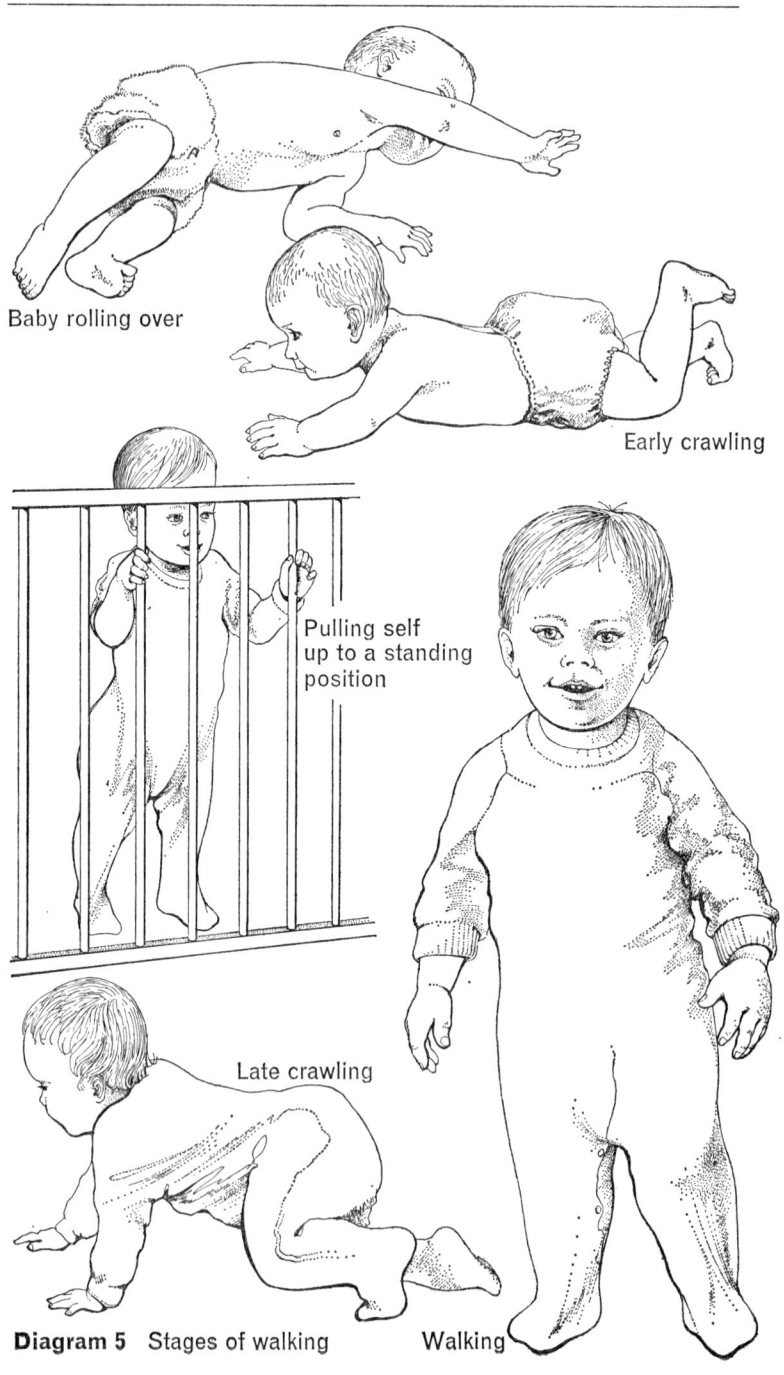

Baby rolling over

Early crawling

Pulling self up to a standing position

Late crawling

Walking

Diagram 5 Stages of walking

Very many parents feel alarm during this period, and for good reason. Immobility in a very small baby invites a feeling of security which is severely shaken by his new command of movement. There are a large number of arrangements which they suddenly need to revise. The drop side of the drop-side cot cannot be left lowered at all. Rooms have to be re-categorized as safe and dangerous: kitchens and bathrooms in particular are often dangerous for a mobile baby. Some jobs, such as ironing, may have to be done when the baby is asleep.

Protection of ornaments is also a real problem. Baby sitters need to be warned that what they had looked on as an easy job, now demands much more vigilance. Older children will need to be reminded not to leave their treasured possessions within range of their hitherto harmless companion.

The start of a very long period has begun. This is the time when a mother has to take all kinds of measures to protect her baby, whose curiosity and range of movements are constantly increasing, but whose understanding of what the consequences of his actions might be remains very low for a matter of years.

One danger is that parents will shout 'No!' and expect understanding to spring from it. Parents would not be human if they did not shout 'No!' occasionally, especially when they suddenly remember some safety measure that they have forgotten. At this same age (about nine months), most children do in fact start to register something of the meaning of this word. But it would be utterly mistaken to suppose that a baby can generalize from this; or perceive *why* the word is used; or realize from hearing it once in association with an object, that this object must not be touched when it is seen again the next day. Apart from expecting too much from conditioning a baby to the word 'no', some parents mistakenly over-use it, with the result that over time one of the clearest associations their children develop is *not* between 'no' and dangerous things, but between 'no' and mother or father. It is a useful word, which inevitably comes into vocabulary early on, but which can have unfortunate consequences for future development of family relations when it is overdone: *expecting* that a parent is more likely to be about to issue a prohibition than anything else cannot be desirable. There are ways of stopping a baby from moving towards harm—distraction, picking him up bodily and laughing, and so forth—which make prohibitions unnecessary. But this requires imagination and a cool head.

The first steps that a baby makes are likely to be along the side of a cot or a settee, when he has levered himself up, or been placed there. One foot sidles round another, while hands clutch at the next point of the furniture. At one point the baby is likely to collapse. Because this is an early experience of baby falling to the ground, mothers rush up in alarm. It is rare, however, for them to come to harm when they collapse, because they naturally go limp. A cushion or two, strategically placed, can be recommended to reduce the numbers of 'eggs' that appear on baby's head.

When he seems to be happy about trying to put one foot in front of the other on his own, he might consent to try it when you yourself are holding both his hands. If he is very suspicious, or clearly alarmed, it is completely pointless to insist. By the time he is ten months old, he is likely to enjoy the idea, and will soon be able to take little walks with you, provided you do not prolong them beyond a few paces. However, some babies who are used to the idea of having at least one hip supported against furniture, may feel dubious about trusting the weight of their bottom to their legs. This seems to apply particularly to babies who have started moving around the house by 'bottom shuffling'. They should certainly not be forced to try to walk properly before they are ready. As with swimming, a shock or a fright at this stage may put them off for a long while. Being late means very little to eventual skill and enjoyment in walking or running.

Some mothers in the past used to stop their babies from walking too early—either by *not* going for little walks with them, or even by forcing them to sit down again if they seemed to be standing or moving along on their feet. Their reason was fear of encouraging bow-leggedness or rickets, by allowing them to take their weight on their legs prematurely. In fact, a healthy baby is most unlikely to suffer in either way, assuming he is not chronically under-nourished.

Some babies may continue to be much more interested in crawling. This is not a kind of movement that every baby needs to achieve at a high standard before progressing to walking. It can be missed altogether—without any apparent effect on later development. For the crawler, though, there is a kind of advance in technique, that can be described as starting like a walrus, and ending like a bear. The very first crawling movement may be walrus-like, with the hands and arms working overtime, pulling a rather reluctant body along. Then the knees work independently, and more efficiently. After about a month, the baby will use the edge of his feet, as well as knees and hands. Later still, when he uses the soles of his feet, his bottom is hoisted higher into the air, and he really does pad around (between about a year and 15 months) rather like a little bear. The advance from one kind of crawling to the next is, it will be noted, 'cephalocaudal'. Only the more determined crawlers get as far as this stage of the act, however. If they do, they might be difficult to contemplate at it very closely, for any length of time. They work up a very impressive speed, which often seems more like scampering. Because they can by now sit upright for as long as they choose, they will not need to stay in a crawling posture once they have reached their goal. The scampering of a two-year-old, or even a three-year-old who steadfastly refuses to change to walking, sometimes has to be seen to be believed. Since many mothers are (unnecessarily) worried and regretful about late walking, these babies' very real athletic achievements usually go unrecognized.

The delight of a parent when, led by both hands, a baby lurches for his first pace or two, is supremely evident. This, rather than any personal sense of greater power (crawling being, after all, *much* easier and much more useful at this point) is the baby's main incentive to go further. Not only is it a shared activity which he values, but it gives pleasure to his mother and his father, and it also gives rise to lashings of praise. Everyone by this age, and earlier even, is very responsive to encouragement of a flattering kind.

Babies can also sense impatience, bad temper, and worry. The fact that these can only be vague feelings for them do not make them any more welcome. Being laughed at is not appreciated by a baby either: he seems to be able to distinguish between being laughed *with* and being laughed *at* by about this time, and shows it in his reactions. None of these things is going to help him to walk more quickly. They are likely to slow him down, and they will certainly reduce his enjoyment both of walking, and of learning things with his parents. On the other hand, being praised promptly and often, will contribute greatly both to success and to enjoyment.

We should now review what lies within the power of the one-year-old. He has learnt to sit up from a lying position, and while sitting up he can do all kinds of things without overbalancing. He is likely to have reached one of these points:

(a) He has begun, and mastered crawling *or*
(b) He has taken to shuffling around on his bottom *or*
(c) He has crawled a bit, but switched his attention to walking, gradually needing less and less support.

While some babies will have spontaneously got the idea of launching out on their legs on to the open floor, and will be walking unaided in their tenth month, this is rather unusual. It is more likely, at one, that a baby will have made a start round the furniture, and be about to allow his parents to lead him around by one hand instead of two. Even if he cannot walk by himself, he may be able to stand alone for a few seconds. Sometimes a baby will do this without realizing it, through being distracted by something else: then he looks down, and drops in dismay. This is a sign that he is *not* entirely confident to walk, and should certainly not be hurried. He can still be praised, even if he drops in a heap. The one-year-old may well have noticed stairs, if they exist in his home. The first crawling movements up the stairs can be expected now—which means that he should not be left unattended at the bottom, or at the top.

The average age at which babies begin walking without any support or helping hand is 15 months. But this is an average that has a wide range of variations—all for perfectly normal and healthy children—on either side. By the time a child is two years old, he might still be stubbornly pursuing other methods of getting around. This is no reason in itself for concern. What a parent of such a child should try to notice, however, is whether he shows other signs of being behind his age group. Is he beginning to show understanding of what is said to him? Can he pick up and play with toys in an assured way? Can he do most of the work of feeding himself? Does he show good balance when he sits up? Does he have effective means of propelling himself around? It is if he is failing in *most* of these respects, and others like them, that qualified paediatric help may be needed. But in any event, as with other worries touched on in this book—*if* you are anxious, talk to your health visitor, your clinic doctor or your family doctor.

Chapter seven
Speech

It is very difficult for an adult to imagine a world in which speech is lacking. The closest one gets to it is perhaps the first arrival in a foreign country where you have not got even a few words on which to build communication. A child who is unlucky enough to have a speech defect may feel some of that helplessness a lot of the time. Developing the ability to express thoughts and to turn them into words is certainly one of the most important aspects of a baby's growth. But although a baby can be helped and encouraged in this, he cannot be *hurried*.

When he is born, a baby cries, but does not make speech noises. The latter ('vocalizations') come into his repertoire towards the end of the first month, starting with occasional sounds that are 'throaty' but recognizably different from cries. Gradually a range of vocalization is produced, often in imitation of mother's voice. This is the basis of components which can be put together more and more accurately to form speech. Clearly this is harder for a deaf baby, who may produce a narrower range of vocalization *at random*, as opposed to getting better and better at imitating and repeating sound patterns. At birth, the structure of the mouth and the chamber below it are not yet right for speech. Maturation, therefore, is needed, as well as learning. To start with, the mouth is too short a distance away from the larynx for any more than a small set of different sounds to be produced when the vocal chords are used. Between the mouth and the larynx is a chamber called the pharynx. This has to expand, relative to the rest of the vocal equipment, in order that it can become an active adaptor of sounds. In advanced vocalization, and in speech itself, the pharyngeal muscles are extensively used, along with the lip and tongue muscles. There have to be rapid changes in the size and shape of the pharynx as air is sent through it from the larynx to the mouth. The range of notes that comes from a clarinet would be impossible to achieve with an instrument only two-thirds the proper size: this is a very imprecise parallel, but it gives some idea of what has to happen.

In the newborn baby, the mouth–pharynx–larynx sequence is not unlike that of an ape. Interestingly, the human baby is the only animal who develops a large and versatile pharynx in this way. Even if he were more intelligent, an ape cannot be taught speech for this reason.

The central nervous system has to mature, too. In the brain there is a particular centre, usually on the left side, which controls the movements of the body that are required for speech, just as there are similar 'motor' centres nearby which control other movements. It takes time for the control to be organized.

Reference was made in Chapter 2 to the idea of 'conative drive', whereby a baby applies his energy and attention to certain things—according to what pleases him, and to how much energy he has. The point was made that natural limits to his conative drive means that a baby cannot develop at the same speed on all fronts at once. Speech is notorious for being liable to be held up for a long time, while progress is being made elsewhere—notably at standing and walking. Very often a baby may seem to be coming along very capably with his vocalization—until he reaches a repertoire of, say, 'da', 'ba', and 'no'—and then there is a period of several months over which no further advance is made at all. This is perfectly common, and understandable in that he is pursuing other things.

Here it is worth noting that although *you* may feel frustrated during this time, since you want to be able to share more conversation with him than simply baby talk, *his* priorities may be quite different. He may feel that the attention he gets and the communication he makes are perfectly adequate: his goal may be to move as quickly as his elder brother (or as quickly as you, for that matter) in order to be the first to reach interesting toys and other objects.

A normal baby will make a fair number of vocalizations when he is three months old—either when someone is perched over him, cooing or talking, or when he is simply by himself and contented with the world. His progress here is matched by increased sensitivity to small differences in sounds. He was always alarmed by a sudden bang. Now, at three months, he will react to, say, two wooden blocks being tapped against each other, in the corner of the room. He may stop what he is doing when he hears this, and pay attention for a second or two. There is an obvious need for interplay between vocalizing and hearing: you cannot get better at the former without getting better at the latter too (see Table 7).

Between three and six months a change comes about in his communication of pleasure. The early squeals of delight when he sees his mother give place to outright laughter. He may well have a good hearty laugh by four months.

The sound of the human voice has had two effects on him from birth. Ignoring a loud or angry human voice for the moment, the baby has had his attention attracted by it, and has been calmed by it. (This does not always work, but the tendency has been there.) Gradually, between three months and six months, he identifies a particular voice—usually that of his mother. If the nursery has several people in it, all talking quietly, and his mother suddenly talks in the doorway, the six-month-old baby will usually show that he has distinguished her particular voice, by looking around and towards the door. This is another important stage so far as speech is concerned, because it shows a degree of discrimination of tone and rhythm.

Some experiments with different types of children who were starting to speak showed that a normal child reacts in a distinctive way to tape recorded speech of people he knows well. Often (when he understands you) he will identify the speakers correctly. The normal child usually learns to speak without difficulty, and this hearing skill suggests that part of this learning is noticing differences in sound qualities. Autistic children, on the other hand, who have great difficulty in learning to speak, often do not show that they recognize individual voices on the tape recorder. They sometimes recognize their *own* voice, however, although this is hard for the normal child. There may be an implication here about the kind of sound perception needed to develop speech properly— and a hint that undue attention to one's *own* vocal production may be restrictive.

At six months, the baby is already putting together some of his vocal syllables. He may favour 'a-do', for example, instead of a simple 'da'. Some of these double syllables are produced in certain contexts, but he will not be entirely consistent in the way that he uses them. They may have some meaning for him, but it is likely to be variable. He is at a stage when language is in flux.

Although much of the time he may be getting more precise in his use of sounds, and he will develop favourites which he repeats, he recognizes no law which says they cannot be changed, or that a noise must mean a particular thing, and not something else. His sounds mean whatever he *wants* them to mean.

Inevitably, however, some phrases that he hears, and which he may use himself, acquire a particular meaning for him. This may come about because they are peculiar to one person or because they are used only in a certain context. Obvious examples of this are 'Dada' and 'Mama'. Curiously, 'Dada' may be recognized and used by the baby earlier than 'Mama', sometimes to his mother's annoyance. This is partly because *d*s and *t*s are slightly easier for him to use, and partly because his mother is there more often, and nobody refers to her by name as often as she refers to his father, when he comes in. Whether he knows the meaning of such words at once is very doubtful. By the age of nine months, the baby will quite possibly be using both names, but imprecisely. He will probably understand 'bye-bye', too, but only a very precocious child will use it correctly. Favourite pets and toys may receive very simplified names from him and (especially if his mother encourages it) he will delight in using them. Although a mother often apologizes for baby language—e.g. ' "Tee-tee"—that's his name for the kitten, I'm afraid'—it is very often her justifiable pleasure at his attempts to say 'kitten' that lead to something like 'Tee-tee' being a long-enduring name. It is, in fact, as much *her* name for kitten.

At this age a lot of talking is babbling. It is sometimes making a point, it is sometimes repeated simply for the amusement of the sounds, or the pleasure of babbling as such.

As he gets older, the baby will shift from a ratio of, say, ten babbling sessions to one situation where he makes an attempt at drawing attention or conversing, to a ratio which is entirely different. Much later, many children may still persevere with little babbling sessions of their own, in which they may repeat over and over again meaningless phrases or rhymes that serve no purpose but to please them. But this could be in regressive moments, when they feel a need to retreat back in time to an age when all talking was fun, instead of being functional.

One sound takes precedence over others towards the end of the baby's first year. This is when he realizes that each time an approach is made towards him, a particular word is used. This can be his name, or his nickname. When a mother is in the habit of calling him 'darling', instead of 'Tom', then Tom may respond to 'darling' more quickly. But whatever it is, a one-year-old will usually show that he knows the name by which he is usually called. If he hears it by chance across the room, he will turn towards the voice that spoke it.

His control over his mouth and lips has increased to the point where, if you listen to his babbling, you can pick out more vowel sounds, and many more consonants than he used before. Certain consonants may continue to elude him for a long time—usually 'r' and a soft 's'—although some babies do not seem to be troubled even by these difficult ones. This depends both on the relative speed at which different children develop precision in their mouth movements, and on the degree to which they will be satisfied by getting close to a sound, as opposed to reproducing the exact sound. While this last point could be a matter of personality, it must also be dependent on the way in which parents 'reinforce' their babies' early speech habits—by nodding each time and repeating early attempts back at him instead of using adult speech. I would not for a moment suggest that parents should be the least bit discouraging when their baby is holding forth—the more encouragement, in fact, the better—but if they show delight in 'babbit' for 'rabbit', and refer to 'babbit' themselves, they are helping postpone the emergence of the true 'rabbit'.

Does this *matter*? In the short run, no. But when parents help prolong early nursery sounds a long way into childhood and then get worried at their child's apparent slowness, they can set up emotional problems, as well as making early social contacts with other children rather more difficult for their son because he 'sounds different'.

At one year, it is interesting to note how many objects and concepts he actually recognizes when words alone are used. Put a ball and a rattle in front of him, and say 'ball'. A month or so back, it would have been a matter of chance which he reached for. Now, however, he is likely to know. The exciting fact about this is that the number of times he has to hear a word before he associates it with an object is decreasing all the time. Of course, this depends on the word (how distinctive it is), and on the object (what interest and importance it has for him). But all kinds of learning with words is speeding up. While it is fair enough to check what he knows, trying to teach him long lists of vocabulary is both unnecessary and unfair: it is making learning the main purpose of your contact.

This development has been largely in terms of *recognition* of words. Some children at this age, even, will be repeating a number of the words themselves, and getting them right a lot of the time. But others, the majority, will find recognition much easier than reproduction, which may be limited to a few very common and simple words.

At this time, exploration by crawling, standing, and (for some) learning to move along the side of a table on their feet, are all occupying a great deal of attention. It can be the period referred to above, when one baby seems to hang back, and learn very little more by way of words to *use*, although there is growth in understanding.

The development from this point towards normal speech is very different from one child to another. One mite at 18 months will be able to hold quite a lengthy conversation with an adult who seems pleasant enough to talk to. Admittedly, there will be a lot of 'jargon' in the speech he uses: that is, some words will be distorted, or repeated in a way that is individual to him, but they will be applied meaningfully, and more or less logically, following their own rules. There is often a remarkable rhythm to the speech of these early talkers—as if they had been struck and fascinated by the lilt of normal adult speech. They seem to pick up this lilt quicker, even, than the considerable vocabulary they have built up.

Another child, who in the fullness of time may prove to be no less intelligent at home or at school, will choose other ways of communicating. He will have a few words, perhaps, but will use them sparingly. If he wants something, he may shout, cry, or take his mother's hand and pull it in the right direction. Not being able to talk may not seem to bother him in the least. His parents may start worrying, and think of him alternately as stubborn or stupid. Neither may be accurate. It is possible, in the case of some late talkers that a lot of their basic needs are anticipated by observant parents, who give them plenty of attention and reduce the actual need to talk. This does not explain all such cases, but is probably a factor in many.

Sir Winston Churchill is supposed to have produced his first words when he was nearly four. His subsequent progress shows that parents can worry too much about lateness in talking. A late talker who is communicating in some way or other, who enjoys others' company, and who is clearly not deaf, is usually just taking his time. If one of these does not apply, special help is probably needed.

Some late talkers seem to wait until they can string together a few words, in mini-sentences, before letting forth. A child who eventually took a first class honours degree in science at Cambridge worried his mother by seeming to have only very rudimentary language up to the age of two-and-three-quarters. He would never ask for something by name if he could possibly avoid it, and never volunteered words or phrases. Since he could understand what he was asked, and he could point to the potty if he needed it, this was less disturbing than it might have been, but it was a worry, none the less. Then, one morning in the kitchen, he solemnly regarded his mother who was staring into the pantry, trying to decide what shopping was needed. 'What are you looking at, Mummy?' he asked. He was never a chatterbox, but progress was rapid after that.

There *is* evidence that early talking tends to go hand-in-hand with greater intelligence. But these examples illustrate the point that this is a *tendency*, not a *rule*. There is plenty of variation on either side. What would be more to the point, probably, is evidence of understanding, at successive ages, and how this ties in with later proofs of intelligence. But standardizing tests of this kind for babies is extremely difficult, since understanding may depend so much on accent, tone of voice, context, and attention.

If a parent finds that his child is particularly late on any of the points in the list in Table 7, it is worth bearing in mind that understanding is a great deal more important than developing fluency of speech early in life. If there is real worry, this is worth discussing at the local children's clinic, or with a doctor—preferably *not* in the child's presence. Doctors often talk about the shudder they feel when an anxious mother enters their room with a toddler in a push-chair, announcing loudly 'I'm worried about Ian because he simply doesn't seem to understand anything'. Ian may not understand precisely the point that is being made, but he will get *something* out of it, and it won't help him one scrap.

If a child is seriously backward in speech, it is usually possible for an experienced clinician to tell whether this is likely to be for physical or emotional reasons, or—which is not uncommon—for a combination of these two. If deafness is suspected as a contributing factor, there are tests which can be made: these are *far better* administered by an experienced medical person. When emotional disturbance is concerned, the clinician has to balance several factors in mind before making up his mind: many normal children are eccentric—is this one more so than could be expected from his experience? Many normal children develop different skills at different rates—is this one also simply a case of being a 'late normal'? Then, there are a number of special types of perceptual handicap that come disguised, with an overlay of behaviour problems (such as autism, where speech is hard but not impossible to develop). Does this child seem to fit into one of these categories? Is he alarmed by the visit to the clinic, and how responsible would this be for apparent disturbance? Does his behaviour build up in the clinician's mind a pattern of anxiety, suppressed aggression, or whatever, that increases consistently from one visit to another?

These are not easy questions, and obviously experience is important. An anxious parent is advised to ask for help—before she gets more anxious. But too much examination, month after month, is not to be recommended. A doctor may feel that a speech therapist should be consulted: this possibility is best discussed with a doctor in the first instance, since he will be considering both whether there is a real problem at all, for he knows more about the child, and whether it is suitable for a speech therapist or not.

As a very general rule, if a child is slow to learn to talk, the prime rule must be—not to be impatient. If he suggests that his understanding is increasing, either of what others are saying, or of situations in general, that is a very good reason for waiting. On the other hand, if his understanding seems to be very slow as well, or stuck, or strangely limited to certain matters and not others, and if his behaviour seems backward in general, this is reason enough for seeking qualified help.

Table 7 shows the stages that the average child reaches and passes at different ages. There is a wide range around the average, particularly from twelve months onwards.

Table 7 Growth of speech

'Pre-speech' is used here to group together functions and abilities which contribute to speech development. Only key points are included: many gestures are omitted.

	Pre-speech	Speech
	Cries and screams from birth.	
1 month	Exchanges looks with mother. Starts 'vocalizing'— (different sounds from crying or screaming). Smiles at mother.	
2 months	Smiles at mother and at others too. Looks towards whoever has just started speaking.	
3 months	Understands reassurance in words or tone in mother's voice. Vocalizes to whoever speaks to him—or pleases him.	
4 months	Laughs out loud. Uses recognizable syllables in his vocalizations.	
6 months	'Asks' to be picked up, by holding out his arms. Responds to his name. Starts to imitate sounds.	
9 months	Pulls at clothes, and/or shouts for attention, or when annoyed, etc. Responds to single words: e.g. no, goodbye.	Uses these recognizable words in a meaningful way.

78 Speech

	Pre-speech	Speech
1 year	Uses most vowels and consonants in vocalizations. Shows understanding of phrases and (single) orders.	Vocalizations become more definite 'jargon' varying according to meaning both in syllables and intonation. Words occasionally stand out in this.
1½ years	Understanding of words, phrases and intonations increases rapidly.	Jargon sounds 'more like conversation'. Uses up to 25 words with meaning (more *without* or with vague meaning). A few phrases (some partly jargon; others entirely words—e.g. wannum bikit mum-mah *or* want a biscuit mummy).
2 years		Uses up to 60 words with meaning. Uses personal pronouns —I, you, etc., and uses own name. Most speech becoming clear, jargon decreasing.
3 years		Vocabulary range very elastic. Increasingly normal, intelligible and 'intelligent' conversation.

Chapter eight

The second year

When a baby is a year old, he deserves his first birthday party. Not that he will understand it as such. But his parents will be proud of the date, and will enjoy it as a special event. Anything that a baby sees his parents enjoying becomes special for him too.

'Twice the child's age, plus one' is the rule of thumb for how many children to have at a birthday party. At one year, this leaves you with precisely one birthday boy and two guests. The babies will not play with each other, although they will note each other's presence, with curiosity and possibly approval, and they will be excited by decorations, new toys, and the candle on the cake. Very likely at least one of them will get too excited. Hence the wisdom of the old rule, limiting the numbers of those who may have to be calmed down to three. A very simple party, at this age, goes a long way.

Here is a typical party that I observed and have embellished only slightly. It is a good moment to watch three one-year-olds, and to see what they are like. Already there are big differences in their development, although all three could not be called anything other than normal. (By coincidence, they are all the same age!)

Frances

She is a fast mover. She has been crawling effectively for the past four months. Now she can scramble from one side of the room to the other. The first thing she does, or release from her push-chair, is to move along the wall of the hallway, supporting herself against it as she walks. Reaching the doorway into the party room, she drops with a bump, rather heavily, but without apparent harm, and canters on all fours to the end of the room where there is a low table, with three toddlers' chairs around it, surmounted by an iced sponge cake with a candle. If somebody is not there at precisely this moment, Frances's inquisitive lunge will carry her straight into the middle of the cake.

She doesn't mind being lifted down, particularly if it is done with good humour. (It happens all the time in *her* house.) She says 'Ooh!' often and delightedly, at everything and anybody. She beams at Tim, whose party it is, although she does not actually play with him.

In fact, she does not spend long on anything in particular. She gives the impression she is too curious about life to concentrate on any specific point of it for too long. But what she likes, she *comes back to*, every so often. She reminds you rather of a cat who is forbidden to sit on a chair and finds twenty ways of returning to the attempt. When she has been removed from the edge of the cake for the fifth time, Tim's mother makes a note that party food should be kept out of the way until its moment of glory has arrived.

Frances sees a mother leaving the room, and makes a flapping noise with her hand, shouting 'ay-ay!' for 'bye-bye'. This is part of her repertoire, and anything at all like the appropriate moment is turned into a chance to use it. She laughs happily when the mum replies 'bye-bye, Frances!' to her.

She gives occasional shrieks of delight when she sees toys on the floor she has not yet seen. Sometimes she will make a lot of 'vocalization' noises, at toy or baby alike, and will be specially pleased if she is noticed.

At tea-time, she shows that she believes feeding to be the equivalent of total immersion. Tim's mother has produced a smooth fruit mixture, in a plastic plate, for each of the babies. Frances can use a spoon, and can get some of the food actually inside her mouth, but she likes using *both* hands, and is a generous distributor of what she grabs. When she consents to be fed by her mother, who is standing by, she fares rather better. But she regards it as hilarious entertainment first, sustenance second. She burrows into her piece of birthday cake like an energetic mole.

After tea, she races from her chair at a scramble to reveal a broad pool. She shows not the slightest awareness of her state. Her mother has wisely judged that since Frances rarely notices what is going on inside her, she is not at all ready for introduction to the potty in any systematic way.

After her nappy change, Frances launches herself into the

party again. But she is less eager now, and when she picks something up, she drops it, with an irritated look. The toys and other babies no longer please her. She sits down, and howls. Her mother has anticipated this, and hovers nearby. A glove puppet, activated by her mother's hand, appears before Frances. She is still crying, but looks at the strange creature with interest. When she is suddenly tickled by it, she gives a yell of laughter, and for a moment is actually laughing *through* her tears, April-wise. Then she gets picked up for a cuddle by her mother, and all is well. She is still tired, however, and needs to be taken home.

Tim

He is another kind of one-year-old entirely. He is two inches longer than Frances, although you cannot tell this because he is usually sitting down, looking around at the world, while Frances is usually in movement. He has a larger head, but a sturdy body. His shoulders are now straight, although he still tends to have the lower part of his back in a curve. He was slow sitting up, and even now he does so slowly, as if he might topple over if he were not careful.

He does not enjoy standing up. He is by no means unusual in this. His mother, who has helped him to his feet once or twice, to see how he likes the idea of standing up and moving about with his hands held, wisely held off when he made it plain that he felt safer on his bottom.

Occasionally, he crawls. But only if he sees something he wants, and if it is close at hand. Even then, it is not the mad scamper of Frances; it is a measured lumbering that he produces. By and large, he prefers the world to come to him.

Nevertheless, he looks at everything with a keen eye, and seems to understand a lot of what goes on. This is obvious in the way he holds his hands out for a new present when it comes. The wrapping mystifies him, but he gets some of the sense of the ritual. He stares at the package solemnly for a moment or two, then passes it back, equally solemnly, to his mother. Frances's mother cannot help laughing, but she conceals this to avoid offending him. 'He doesn't seem to like it much,' she comments. (Frances would have grinned and gurgled—at the very least.) But Tim's mother just smiles, because she knows that when her son is being perfectly happy he doesn't always register it.

She opens the present and finds a pyramid of plastic squares, around a central stick. When she hands it to him, he reaches for it, but it is too complicated for him to hold. The plastic squares tumble on to the carpet. 'A-beh' says Tim (the only word he uses) which signifies here that he sees something interesting that he must do. He picks up a square, and pushes it, slowly and thoughtfully, against the stick. It doesn't go on as he supposed, and he then tries putting it on top of one of the other squares. Five minutes later, he is still engrossed in the game. One of the mothers has put one of the squares over the stick, and this principle is being grasped by him, although the idea of putting the squares on *in order* will probably be too hard for several weeks.

He is remarkably dogged in his concentration. He has to be, because his hand movements are still rather clumsy when he is trying to cope with the plastic squares. The stick goes into his mouth in the end, and he chews on it. The first of his molars is coming through, and it irritates him so that he bites on it from time to time.

All at once, without warning, he breaks out into loud sobs. Everybody is rather surprised. His mother, who had disappeared into the kitchen, hurries back and looks at him. 'What's wrong Tim?' she asks quickly. Magically, he stops crying, glances at her, then picks up the stick and seems to ignore her again. For a moment, there had been two mothers and two other babies in the room, making a lot of noise while a new record was on the nursery gramophone. His mother wasn't there, and despite being in his own home, he became alarmed.

He is quickly himself again, and makes his way purposefully across the floor to where another mother is sitting. He is attracted by the short white stick between her fingers that is red at one end, and has a blue curling thing above it. Just in time, it is whisked away from his enquiring hand. Tim's parents don't smoke: but even if they did, at this stage in his life Tim would be more curious than prudent. Neither he, nor Frances, nor his other guest Peter, have any concept of danger beyond a very crude association of certain prohibitions with certain situations. Frances, for example, has learnt not to grab for her mother's cigarette, but cannot relate this to avoidance of anything smoking or hot.

At tea, Tim is put out because they are proposing to eat in the sitting-room instead of the kitchen, and because his regular spoon is in someone else's place. He allows himself to be talked around by his mother, but is suspicious until eating actually begins. He is a stickler, already, for order. When eating, he is very different from Frances. He proceeds methodically through everything, refuses help, and makes a good job of independence.

The candle-lighting delights him. But he doesn't understand blowing out the match, and although encouraged to blow out the candle, too, he suddenly feels the eyes of the world upon him, and refuses to co-operate.

Later, he is seen chewing the candle reflectively, while his guests are leaving. He doesn't return Frances's wave, but he looks in her direction. His mother suspects he has had enough of visitors for the time, and is glad they are going.

Peter

He did not seem to enjoy the party much. On arrival, he cried, because he disliked the look of the house and the suggestion that his outdoor clothing would be removed. In fact, Peter loves going out in his push-chair. Stopping at the party was an uncalled-for interruption of one of his favourite enjoyments.

Pacified, and put down on the sitting-room floor, Peter at once puckers his face and prepares to howl his disgust. He is picked up, and stays put on his mother's lap for half-an-hour, with his thumb stuck into his mouth. He looks around him in a way that suggests defensiveness. When anyone approaches he snuggles closer to his mother, and tries to avoid anyone touching him.

Frances comes up once or twice, beams at him, and shakes a wooden ring with bells in front of him. He gives her a look that embarrasses his mother because it is so unfriendly. Actually, Frances doesn't care at all.

Just when his mother is beginning to think they might really just as well have stayed at home—it was no comfort to watch the *other* children enjoying the occasion—Peter puts out his hand and says 'go-go'. This phrase is overworked in Peter's vocabulary: here it means, quite distinctly, 'I want to get down'. Sensibly, his mother gets down on all fours with him, so he can keep her in view while he makes for the humming top that attracted his gaze.

He had noticed it when it was spun for Tim. But he has waited until the coast was clear before striking out for it. Only a month or two before, the top while spinning and humming would have been a different thing from the same top when it is still. Tim and

Frances, even, might not appreciate that that colourful static thing might be so used as to become that humming spinning top that had amazed them. In fact, Peter is quite advanced in the way he concentrated on the object as it passed from one state into the other, and approached it clearly with the aim of encouraging it to perform again.

His movements towards it are fun to watch. He has only just begun to balance on his own two feet without his hand being held. He plants his two feet wide apart, his bottom (accentuated by a voluminous nappy) is held behind his centre of gravity, and with his head held foremost, and swinging his arms, he achieves a precarious balance. When he stops by the top, his knees bend, and he sits straight down without moving his feet. It looks to be quite a bump: but Peter is well padded, and used to it.

'Go-go' he now says to the top, and to his mother, whom he sees next. He puts his hand out and pats the handle. A month or so back, he would probably have put his head forward, and tried to get the handle in his mouth.

His mother sets the top spinning, and Peter is delighted. The sound attracts Frances, who scampers up and shrieks at it, in a mixture of pleasure and imitation. Peter dislikes this, and makes sure Frances does not come between him and his mother.

It is tea-time. Frances is summoned, and she goes immediately. Peter wants the top to go again, but his mother puts it away in the toy box, and carries him across the room. Later, after tea, he goes up to the toy box and finds the top very quickly. (Again, this shows he is ahead at understanding that objects are 'constant', whether they are put away or not.)

He is bothered by the idea of sitting up to this strange table, and refuses everything. 'It's like trying to feed a plastic gnome in the garden', his mother comments apologetically. The other mothers do indeed wonder if Peter is not a little unsociable. But each thinks in terms of her own child. It is extremely common for a baby to shine at home, but not away, and the whole concept of being sociable or not is premature. To try to insist that a baby fit in with the party would be both self-defeating and unkind: it would probably, in fact, put the baby on his guard against such events in the future.

Peter is taken back across the room, sat on his mother's lap again, and offered some jelly. This he accepts. In fact, he hasn't got to the point of wanting to feed himself at all. He will play with a spoon, and he will poke, with a curious finger, into his bowl. But he sees no point in doing his mother out of the job. And there is no point in pushing him into it.

While chewing reflectively on a piece of apple (provided by Tim's mother instead of sweets or chocolate biscuits) Peter suddenly stops, looks at his mother in a particular way, and repeats 'go-go'—with a different intonation from before. His mother rises swiftly, and carries him to the bathroom, where she is not quite quick enough to prepare him for sitting on a potty, but able to avoid getting wet, or leaving him wet before changing him. At home, she has been able, more and more often, to get him to sit on the potty and perform in it, after getting a signal from him. At first, this was impossible, because the signal was simultaneous with the act. But now (rather early at 12 months) Peter communicates his needs a little before the event. It takes a skilled interpreter to understand him, of course. By not fussing about it, and by paying him elaborate compliments when it works, she has helped Peter enjoy this part of life, and to be happy about co-operating.

The other mothers are rather impressed by this. They put their babies on the potty as a general encouragement to come to like it, rather than in expectation of results. But, wisely, they are not anxious to make an issue out of toilet training.

It should be obvious that each of these mothers has, in fact, got a baby whose progress in some respects is advanced, and in others is a little slow. Because I know these children, I can add that they each seem very ordinary (in a *good* sense) and very appealing in their personality. The mothers may sound a bit too perfect: they would be the first to admit mistakes, but to an outsider these always seem to be on trivial matters, not on anything important.

Frances's mother is delighted to have a child who moves in a way that is athletic, confident, and who promises to be very friendly and outgoing. Tim's mother and father sometimes talk to each other about when he is going to start walking (especially when they have just seen Frances) but they admire the way he concentrates on toys or problems, and the way he uses his fingers. Peter's mother feels she has a clinging vine instead of a son, sometimes, but is proud of his walking, and the way he communicates so much to her, even with a very few syllables. She feels he will talk very soon, and she is probably right.

Over the coming year, each child is going to advance a great deal. There are many ways in which this will be obvious. Underlying them, is the fact that their *brain* is continuing its rapid growth. Between the ages of six months and two and a half years, the size of a child's brain increases from a weight of about half to a weight of three-quarters of an adult's brain. Nobody understands the brain fully, but it is clear from experiments with animals, and from studies of children in developing countries that protein nourishment, and stimulation from others of the same kind—particularly the mother—are very important in the first year of life for the cells of the brain to multiply at a normal rate. We can guess that this must mean that connections in the brain increase rapidly during this time, to allow understanding, the forming of intentions, and the control over the rest of the body that gets the intentions put into practice. The second year has been shown by doctors working with impoverished tribes to be rather less important as a time when nourishment has to reach a high minimum for the brain to be able to grow properly. But nourishment is obviously still needed, and an attentive parent is almost vital for the brain to learn to be used.

In this second year, with stronger mental equipment, most babies will:

Become 'toddlers' They will abandon crawling for walking, and will lose the need for a hand to be held. Some show their dependence (and love) by refusing to walk *without* a helping hand—and even get annoyed with themselves when they find they have been tempted to go solo. Some will climb stairs, and run almost as soon as walking. But the average target date for running is two years. (See Table 6.)

Start talking Gradually the vocalizations become grouped into standard phrases that fit certain situations and certain meanings. Some will sing as well. (Usually, this is if mother sings too, and if there is plenty of song music in the house.) Not very polished, but delightful. By two years, a baby may have words, although some very intelligent ones will still be silent. (See Table 7.)

Be a self-feeder He will accept more and more of the basic foods the family eats, doing away with the need for baby tins. A food mixer is a step along the way. But by two, he can take 'meat and two veg' if it is chopped up for him. Feeding oneself with a spoon comes first. Spearing objects with a fork is picked up later, and cutting up difficult foods like meat demands a lot of practice and more wrist power than a toddler commands. But he will get along competently with a spoon and fork by two.

Toilet trained (partly)   In the middle of his second year, he may progress from noticing when he is passing water, to informing his mother about it, to telling her when he is *about* to do so. (The same applies to defecation.) The more mobile and self-willed won't bother to tell, but will march to the lavatory, and get into a tangle trying to prepare themselves for the potty. Early talkers sometimes proudly announce the fact that they are producing something: this is often comic, but do *not* make fun of it. One mother I met used to greet the news with 'that's no flaming use to me, then, is it', and a sharp laugh. Two years later, her child was still in nappies. Scolding, or bad-tempered nappy changing can also delay control, as can jealousy of a younger brother or sister (who gets attention through *not* having control). Control through the night at this age is rare. Lapses in control are very common. Late toilet training has no connection with lack of intelligence.

Be a water-baby   Usually before he is twelve months old, a baby starts treating bath-time as something *he* wants to organize—rather than having it functionally arranged for him. Now he becomes much more experimental, kicking, splashing, putting his head under and drinking the water. Some parents have taught their babies to *swim* at this age—it has been argued that it is easier to learn to float and swim *before* walking, i.e. while crawling seems the natural thing to do. Most babies have virtually no fear of water in their second year—which must help. Associating water with pleasure at this age can be a big benefit to future development. Psychologists regard water play as a legitimized form of messing, and a healthy way of expressing emotion, apart from all else. But the greatest care must be taken to avoid situations which will associate water with fear.

Build   After picking things up, dropping and finding them, and hitting things together, comes *putting* things *together*. Building may be too grand a term for many of the operations learnt in the second year. Now that he can use his thumb and fingers without having to get his palm involved, towers of bricks become more of a possibility. Sandcastles are harder, but the principle of getting a firm substance with sand and water together (or mud, for that matter) usually comes by the age of two. He is particularly pleased by *joint* building schemes with mother or father.

Manipulate   As well as for building, a child approaching two develops a keen eye for fitting one object into another, and the finger control he needs for it. A cardboard sheet with a set of coins embedded in appropriate holes is not advisable at one: both because he is scarcely able to lift each coin to put them back, and because he will very likely try them in his mouth and swallow them. But at two he can ease them up, with practice, and see how to put the 50p heptagon into the right heptagonal bed, the round 10p pieces into their beds, and so on. (Stay close in case he *does* try eating them, though.) His pull, and his push both get very much stronger over this period: the proof is the number of toys that are taken apart at this stage, rather than just broken on the floor. He can sometimes withdraw or replace a jam jar top with a screwing motion by two, although this may take him a little longer. The same applies to holding a chalk or crayon and striking out with it. He will soon open doors.

Imitate   The second year is a great copy-cat age. Lots of jobs done round the home by either parent are apt to be copied. Vacuum cleaning, cooking, washing up, making beds, painting, wallpapering—anything that his parents obviously find important to do, are targets for imitation. Three wishes are usually discernible: *to be with* his parents, more, to *join in with* them, and *to do as* they do. The balance of these motivations varies with personality, and family circumstances. Some two-year-olds, for example, make a great show of imitating; others do it quietly, almost unobtrusively; others are happiest when imitating an act that is done on them, e.g. 'feeding mummy', which increases involvement with mother. Elder brothers and sisters are, of course, imitated too, particularly when it is obvious that what they do attracts attention and praise from their parent.

Play games   Imitation becomes obvious in some of the games that a child develops, approaching two years old. Comparing the very simple games of the one-year-old shows what progress is made in the direction of copying, of imagining, and of using trial-and-error as a way of finding out a lot of information. At one, a baby will be starting to drop things and find them again, sometimes making it difficult for himself to do so. Some psychologists believe this can be symbolic of the situation in which the mother leaves and comes back —but with the difference that the baby is in control. Towards two years of age, he is aware of much more that is going on, and has many more frustrations—e.g. *not* to touch this, not to do that, not to go out with his mother this time, and so on. His play is all the richer. He uses toys, and what he does to toys are ways of re-creating problem solutions or enjoyable moments: one toy always comes to bed, one toy is always punished, etc.

Listen to stories   Very simple stories at first. He won't understand them all, and will want them repeated. But as his concentration span for attention gets longer, so he can enjoy sessions with picture books much more.

These are some of the more obvious developments between one and two. They are only symptoms, however, of a more general 'potential', in terms of understanding and being able to act on that understanding, that is increasing all the time. A one-year-old will surprise you sometimes: a two-year-old is *full* of surprises. So watch it!

Some questions that parents ask during their babies' second year

1 He doesn't seem to be able to say words clearly. Sometimes he seems to stammer. Will this get worse? What can I do about it? A very large number of babies have hesitations when they are starting to talk. These result from imprecise motor control over their speech mechanism. Some believe these babies have thoughts that move too fast for them to be able to articulate. The more important it seems for them to get something across, the more they seem to hesitate. Whether this is called 'stammering' or not depends on the listener. It can often be made *worse* (so that everyone calls the result stammering) by drawing the child's attention to it. Some American psychologists refer to stammering as having a 'diagnostic origin': that is, there is no real problem until parents decide there is. The tension they set up between themselves and their child turns a tendency to stammer into a definite handicap. Even saying 'Now, take it easy, start again and remember we've got plenty of time' is liable to be counter-productive. Completely ignoring the 'stammer' is the best strategy with a very young child.

When children start stammering at an older age (after developing speech normally) it is a symptom of other problems—possibly indicating, for example, that toilet training has been too severe.

2 He refuses to eat meat of any kind. What can I do about it? Not much. He probably doesn't like the taste or the texture. There are many other sources of protein—milk, eggs, fish, and cheese, for example—which can be prepared for a one-year-old. Of course, it is inconvenient. But the best course is to ignore it, and leave meat off his menu for a while. Forcing compliance will set him against meat for a long time, probably against other foods as well, and possibly against you.

After a gap, you can subtly introduce small amounts of a kind of meat he's not expecting in a medium he appreciates—a shred or two of chicken mixed up with carrots, perhaps. If it works, you can increase the proportion.

3 He doesn't show any sign of walking, although he's nearly two. Is this abnormal? It is perfectly possible for such a child to continue to refuse to walk for another six months, and still be perfectly normal. He will catch up in due course. If there are any signs of poor motor control, however, he may have some slight handicap. It is worth asking a doctor to make a careful examination to check that this is not the case—but that should suffice. If there *is* a slight handicap, there are a lot of ways that paediatricians can help nowadays.

4 He is still thumb-sucking, late in his second year. Why is this? Is he insecure? Will it distort his teeth? Psychologists argue about thumb-sucking. Traditionally, it is felt to be a symbolic substitute for sucking at the breast. But symbolism is a very sophisticated concept for an infant brain. Children develop a habit of thumb-sucking during their first month, and it often disappears after the first six months. About 50 per cent will have stopped thumb-sucking by twelve months. But with other children it persists even to the age of five or six—usually ending up as a kind of 'fall-back position' for the child when he feels *very* tired or *very* frustrated.

Older children are being regressive when they suck their thumbs. Some prefer several fingers at a time, or part of a blanket. Some hook part of their sleeve over a thumb, and then suck that. There is no reason why they should not, if it comforts them, but if they do it continually, they may have a problem that needs bringing to the surface.

Thumb-sucking will not harm tooth formation—until a child is doing it continuously after the age of six. Even then, the danger is comparatively slight, because so many children's teeth grow asymmetrically anyway.

5 My husband and I often argue about whether we should smack our baby or not. Sometimes, when he is obviously naughty, we feel we have to or he will go on playing up and get worse. Is this right? Or is he too young to be smacked? If you are quick-tempered, and react impulsively to shock or sudden annoyance—for example, if your toddler lobs a tennis ball into your cup of coffee—then you will probably smack him whatever the books say. There is a school of thought that a sharp reaction relieves tension most quickly: a slap is probably better than a black mood lasting several hours. But if you punish, you must expect two things:
   (a) Your baby will take after you. He will regard hitting as an adult means of expression, highly suitable for use against younger children in times of anger.

(b) Your baby will not *understand* the justice you mete out. (What, for example, if the tennis ball *missed* your coffee?) He will feel there is an incalculable side to your nature, which will disturb him because you are the rock which makes the world stable for him.

A smack does no good to a baby in his second year. It may do some (temporary) good to his mother, but it can become a drug. Overwrought mothers sometimes find themselves watching a toddler getting nearer and nearer to the forbidden mantelpiece, saying to themselves 'Just wait till he reaches the clock—then I'll give him what for!' A smack cannot teach a toddler anything—except, indirectly about the *smacker*.

An older child may well bear grudges about punishment. This is one reason why punishment breeds punishment: he looks for ways of exacting revenge which in turn get punished.

What should parents do, then, with a child who seems 'impossible'?

(a) Quickly insist on what you believe to be right. Quiet authority impresses children far more than parents often realize.
(b) Avoid punishment situations. Remember that prohibitions are often not understood in the second year. Provide distractions, and anticipate and remove opportunities for being 'naughty'.
(c) Remember that the vast majority of parents have smacked a baby once or twice, when really at the end of their tether. They have felt guilty, but later relieved that their relationship has survived happily. (Essentially, your baby wants that relationship to survive.)

6 My baby daughter is always playing with herself. Surely she shouldn't at her age? Is it harmful? What should I do about it? The best thing to do is to relax. Masturbation of some kind is almost universal among small children, of both sexes. (Parents naturally forget what *they* did as toddlers.) Many do not play with their genital area much before two and a half years, but thereafter very few do not. The chances of a child doing himself or herself any harm are nil.

When it profoundly embarrasses the grandparents, parents can try distracting a child from masturbation by playing a game like pat-a-cake that involves his hands, or by offering a toy to play with. But drawing the child's attention to what he is doing, and declaring the genitals a prohibited area is likely to:

(a) increase masturbation in secret by giving it the added pleasure of forbidden fruit, and
(b) associate guilt with pleasure from the genitals which encourages long-term difficulties in relationships with the opposite sex.

Chapter nine

What can go wrong?

It is worth considering briefly the main problems that can affect a baby during his first year. Most of this book deals with normal development and with what 'most children' are doing at particular times. This chapter is devoted to some of the most common ways in which this progress can be interrupted. It is *not* a substitute for a medical manual however: Dr Jolly's book is probably the best source for immediate advice on whether to consult a doctor in any particular predicament.

Physical problems

Out of every 100 babies that are born alive, two at the very most have some kind of serious abnormality. Many of these abnormalities can be treated nowadays, and if steps are taken early enough there may be no lasting evidence of it as the child grows up.

There is a very wide range of these abnormalities at birth, so that the chances of any single one occurring in a family are in fact very small. If a noxious drug, however, such as thalidomide, gains currency, the chances are automatically increased.

The hare lip, and the clubfoot are the most frequent abnormalities that are *entirely* physical matters. There are different kinds of clubfoot, but in most cases, either condition can be successfully tackled to minimize speech or walking difficulties.

Blindness and deafness, of course, are always with us. These are sometimes (but *not* always) connected with other problems of brain development. Because both blind and deaf babies cry, enjoy their feeds, and so forth, their condition is not entirely easy to spot. Some are not entirely blind or deaf. They will tend to use the sense which they *have* got in such a way as to compensate for what they are lacking. This, too, makes diagnosis more difficult.

But a deaf child will often be startled by the sudden sight of someone who has walked naturally across the room, up to his cot. The failure of a blind child to exchange looks with his mother by the end of the first month is a significant warning, too.

Nowadays a great deal is known about how to help these physically handicapped children to realize their full potential. There are special schools for the blind and the deaf. There are also schemes to get more integration of handicapped children with normal children. This is important, because keeping them separate leads inevitably to failure of each to understand the other.

The commonest mental handicap that has tangible physical origins is probably mongolism. The mongol child can be extremely friendly, kind, and very good company. Each year some new milestone in teaching mongol children seems to be passed. They are almost unique in having no sexual problems of any kind. They need help, but they are full of surprises—usually nice ones. The local branch of the National Society for Mentally Handicapped Children (NSMHC) will give a great deal of encouragement and practical ideas on how to cope and what kind of plans to make for a mongol child's future.

Another sizeable group are those babies who are born spastic. These have had cerebral palsy, which may affect a slight or a large area of the brain, but especially that part which controls movement. This is the so-called 'motor-area' along one side of the deep fissure that separates the back part of the brain from the front and the sides. Close by, on the other side of the fissure, is the sensory area, receiving signals of how the different parts of the body are moving. Both are probably affected in a spastic child. But there are big variations. Some are highly intelligent, and go to college, while others have a difficult time ahead of them in learning things. Sometimes, spastic symptoms are difficult to diagnose easily, *or*, they get covered up. It depends on the amount of damage to the brain, but also on understanding, great patience, and specialized training. The Spastics Society was set up to help them.

Autism is more common than blindness, but less common than deafness. Children who are blind or deaf sometimes show autistic symptoms. While no one knows for certain what causes it, there is a feeling nowadays that it starts at, or before birth, and is basically a perception problem which makes the world seem a strange place—full of sights and sounds that are difficult to piece together or to recognize. This makes it all seem a puzzling business, trying to cope with it all and fit in with what other people are doing. It is little wonder that they have behaviour problems, which are sometimes very wearing. But when they start learning—and there are now a few schools for them, too—they have shown that they can accomplish great things, and that they can fit in very happily into their family and into society. The National Society for Autistic Children is the group to contact.

Only a very small number of the abnormalities that are present at birth have been mentioned. But as they account for by far the largest proportions I will stop here, rather than produce a long catalogue.

There are also a large group of children born prematurely, who have been described in Chapter 1. Provided they are given the right conditions of a steady temperature, in an infection-free environment, there is little reason why, with the modern methods of feeding that are available in maternity hospitals, they should not develop healthily.

Children seem to be—fortunately—remarkably resistant to most illnesses. Admittedly, they will be set back by an illness, especially when they are still very small, even if it is only the common cold. For a few days, it is as if they are concentrating the whole of their attention and energy to getting rid of the infection that is upsetting them, so that they do not have time for much else. This is putting it rather fancifully—a baby does not choose consciously where to direct his energy—but this is the impression given. Later, unless he has had a prolonged, severe illness, he regains ground very quickly.

This check to progress affects virtually everything, with one important exception. The baby may stop exploring his cot so eagerly, and he may be off his food. He kicks less, enjoys his bath less, and whether he was starting to lift his head up, or to sit right up, he drops back here too. But he is experiencing a new facet of his relationship with his mother, which increases his feelings of security and dependence. A sick baby usually gets more, not less attention, and it is likely that he associates being made comfortable and getting better with his mother.

Almost all of the illnesses that a child contracts in infancy are the result of infection of some kind. He does not develop tuberculosis, for example, because it is 'in the family', or because he has colds or bronchitis that 'gets worse'; he gets tuberculosis from somebody who has the disease himself, and coughs into the atmosphere in which the baby is breathing.

Some illnesses can be prevented by immunization—that is, by giving the baby a vaccine either by injection or through the mouth. Table 8 shows which of the commoner or more dangerous ones come into this category, and which do not. The last two in the left-hand column are in brackets, because it is unusual for doctors to advise immunization against either of them at least until the child is going to school, if at all.

There is also smallpox to be considered, along with tropical diseases—but only in those countries where infection is common, *or* in cases where contact with a sufferer is suspected. A doctor will only advise inoculation where there is a real danger.

Although there is virtually no risk worth speaking of in vaccination nowadays, care is taken not to give a small baby too many things for his system to cope with, too soon after each other. It is very worth while for the parents, as well as the doctor, to keep a careful record of each vaccination their child is given, noting both what it was for, and the time. This means that the information is at hand in case of a sudden move, or an emergency. Inoculation is avoided when a baby has certain skin problems.

Table 8   Immunization

Babies can be vaccinated against	but not against
Diphtheria	Chickenpox
Whooping cough	Scarlet fever
Tetanus	Colds, bronchitis, etc.
Poliomyelitis	
Tuberculosis	
Measles	
Mumps (mainly in USA)	
(German measles; Influenza)	

Two other major illnesses should be mentioned, although they are uncommon. Immunization is not given against meningitis (inflammation of the 'meninges', parts of the head within the skull, lying between the solid matter of the brain) or encephalitis (inflammation of the brain itself). These conditions can both develop independently as illnesses in their own right. They can be treated, but they are very serious. Sight and hearing may be affected, temporarily or permanently, and in some cases there is a mental defect. Obviously, there is always an interruption of development.

The really dangerous illnesses in Table 8 are diphtheria (although thanks to immunization a serious case of it is now very rare in the UK), tetanus and poliomyelitis. But for a child under a year *any* of them can be serious. And for a child under three months (especially a premature baby) even a cold is likely to be serious. Hence the importance of rigorously excluding small babies from contact with anybody who is ill, or known to be in contact with illness. Measles is a big danger, to the weak.

This poses what can be an insoluble problem when a mother returns home from the maternity ward, to find that her husband and her two older children (say, five and three) have all got streaming colds. She cannot barricade herself and her baby in a single room, barring the way to all-comers. It is neither practical, nor desirable where the feelings of the older children are concerned. But the curiosity that the family will show towards the baby should be kept in bounds, so that they are not allowed close to him for more than a moment. Children do, in fact, accept this without getting more jealous of the baby than they would normally become, *if* they are told very simply why they should keep away. Even if they do not fully understand it, they appreciate being given an explanation. Their mother herself may well catch their cold: what should she do? Some doctors advise wearing a gauze mask whenever feeding, changing, or bathing the baby, or doing anything with him close at hand. Others regard this practice as unnecessary, on the grounds that this only decreases the possibility of infection by very little, unless the mother sees the baby only rarely. Probably each mother should listen to her own doctor or clinic's advice on this, and make up her own mind. But when there is a sign that the baby himself may have caught the cold, the doctor or clinic must be informed at once. The older the baby is, the less the cold matters. Some babies seem to catch cold very easily, and frequently, but without any important effect. After six months it is only lasting colds that need to be mentioned to the doctor, unless it seems to you to be severe.

Once a child has reached the age of about $2\frac{1}{2}$, most doctors seem to be resigned to the idea that he should contract a dose of chickenpox, and German measles—spread out over time, of course! The principle is that this avoids contracting at least the first three of these illnesses either when schooling is likely to be interrupted at an important stage, or in adulthood. From the age of about fifteen upward, each of these can be considerably worse in its effects. German measles is not contracted more than once. There is a strong case for immunizing girls against it at puberty. Table 9 shows a typical schedule for immunization.

Table 9 Immunization programme

Before 3 months	No immunization given except if there is a contact with: tuberculosis, smallpox (or if parents visit a country where smallpox is endemic).
In the 6th month	Against poliomyelitis (1st dose). Against diphtheria, whooping cough, and tetanus (the 'cocktail' oral vaccine) (1st dose).
In the 8th month	2nd dose of both the above.
In the 12th month	3rd dose of both the above.
In the 14th month	Against measles.

Note
Practice varies by local health authority.

No protection can be given against accidents—apart from trying to prevent them. The commonest accidents that bring a baby into a hospital are burns and scalds. This gives some idea of the kind of situation that parents tend *not* to foresee. Recurrent burns and scalds, and skin problems in general, can sometimes be signs of emotional distress: usually this is with an older child, but the possibility should not be overlooked in an apparently 'accident prone' child.

Falls, too, can be dangerous, but this depends very much on where a baby lands, on the hardness of the surface, and the height from which he has fallen. A boiling saucepan is *always* a boiling saucepan, and has the same destructive effect on skin tissue.

The worse kinds of falls can lead to fracture of the skull, or to bone fractures. Concussion will probably coincide with the first. But concussion does not necessarily mean that the skull is fractured. Loud crying and anger on the part of the baby are comparatively good signs. Less encouraging is drowsiness. *Anything* suggestive of concussion must be reported to a doctor at once. Bone fractures are sometimes difficult to spot because of a baby's puffiness, but his pain should be obvious. The bone is less likely to be completely broken, than to be bent, possibly with some fibres severed. This is because the bones are growing, and the fracture is called 'greenstick'. The danger for development is that the bones may not grow straight, as they were meant to, but become misshapen in the direction of the break. At a hospital casualty ward, X-rays can be taken, so that the risk of this can be calculated, and guarded against.

Breaks of the skin, for similar reasons, need to be treated carefully to avoid a permanent effect. In general, a cut that is horizontal has a poorer chance of knitting together neatly and invisibly than

Table 10 Problems you should take to your doctor

1	**Vomiting**	When it is more than just a reaction to a fast feed; when it accompanies very loose bowel movements; when there is blood in it.
2	**Eye infections**	
3	**Earache**	Strong suspicion is enough.
4	**Abdominal pain**	Strong suspicion is enough.
5	**Fever**	
6	**Rupture**	Anywhere except at the navel, where the trouble will usually take care of itself, rupture needs treatment.
7	**Hoarse and noisy breathing**	
8	**Obesity**	Consistently gaining weight much more quickly than the general range—see Table 2 on weight and height.
9	**Drowsiness**	After a fall or shock.

a vertical one. This is because gravity is combining with the growth pattern of the skin to throw the opposite 'banks' of the cut further apart, leaving a bigger scar. Methods of stitching used nowadays are better calculated to help the tissues repair in as neat and natural a way as possible.

There are many other problems, most of them temporary, that can beset a baby. As this is not a medical compendium, Table 10 lists some signs that are to be taken seriously and quickly reported.

Most children learn to love animals. They are an enrichment of life, and they allow feelings of care, protection, and responsibility to grow in a child. But some children, every year, are harmed by animals, or frightened by them to the extent that they avoid them or hate them when grown up.

Animals should be kept away from very young babies, and only introduced to them gradually and carefully. For every Nana (who loved and tended the children in Peter Pan) there is one dog who was the centre of attention before the baby's birth, resents his demotion, and takes out his jealousy on the baby. Or there is the old dog who suddenly shows he is older and less tolerant than everybody thought. The same can be said for cats. Both animals are carriers of parasites and can spread infection. A spotless kitchen or nursery, with a dog inside it, is a danger zone. Birds carry infection, too.

A crawling baby will soon find a dog or cat if there is one around—but by this time he is stronger, and is finding as many germs on the floor as on a dog's coat. Babies at this age cannot understand any complicated instructions about petting or stroking, but not pulling at fur. They are curious, and will grab a handful of fur, or poke a finger into a canine mouth or eye. It is expecting far too much of both to leave a baby and dog together unsupervised.

Mental problems

A number of physical symptoms can be mistaken, and accepted at face value, instead of being interpreted as evidence that something is going wrong with a baby's emotional development. Skin problems often have their roots in anxiety. Allergies seem to be more a question of physical cause-and-effect, but are sometimes complicated by psychological factors.

Crying is also a case in point. All babies cry. They do so for various reasons. One is in response to pain or discomfort. One is a demand for food. But both these reasons are incomplete in themselves. A baby crying because the wetness on his nappy is making his bottom feel sore is asking for kindness and attention as well as relief. He is also asking for renewal of the attachment he feels to his mother. This has been touched on already in answer to one of the questions at the end of Chapter 4.

Doctors and psychologists are often suspicious of prolonged crying for no apparent reason. There are different kinds of crying sound: when prolonged crying sounds 'bitter' or 'forlorn' (these descriptions are inadequate, but to an experienced ear they have meaning) there is often found to be a history of neglect. This sounds as if it implies under-feeding, inattention to nappy-changing, and totally failing to provide basic necessities of life and comfort. But neglect can be in terms of time spent enjoying each other's company, too.

Some mothers say of a baby crying loud and long—'He has a time of day at which he *likes* to cry'; or 'He's a howler, that one'; or 'He gets bored easily'. None of these concepts is really satisfactory.

It is quite wrong to imagine that because a baby cannot say clearly what he feels, or because he does not know any other existence, he accepts what he is given by way of a benevolent routine, and simply 'develops'. It is in the nature of a human being to want *more* than the life of a happy vegetable. A baby would be unnatural if he passively accepted a pattern to the day which allowed for so much contact with his mother (or mother-substitute) at set times, for specific events like having a bath. Of course, in the long run, some kind of compromise has to be reached. Life is not total devotion to a baby. But in the first three years of a baby's life, anticipation of repeated bouts of crying through providing for more mother-and-baby-together periods is to give a much more solid foundation for the child to build up future relationships.

Fathers, and other members of the family can help. They provide invaluable distraction at difficult times. No father should be allowed to get away with 'I'm not much good at this—he doesn't seem to like me'. This is an attitude of the father's mind. He cannot be compelled to enjoy his baby's company. But even when he is not demonstratively affectionate by nature, he might be flattered to think that by being with his baby—smiling, talking to him, showing him things, encouraging him, whistling a song to him if he likes—he contributes greatly to his baby's future confidence, *and* (indirectly) to his baby's all-important relationship with his mother. And this is true.

Some fathers develop a view that the nursery is not for them, because they are being shut out by possessive mothers; others because their wives over-sell the pleasures of parenthood, or set up a resistance by accusing them of low enthusiasm. Indifference in a father is very regrettable, and it is very often brought about by *both* parents. An indifferent father needs to be coaxed and encouraged back, not ordered or shamed into it.

It is worth underlining the point about the link between closeness of mother and baby with preparation for meeting others in life, by considering the development of young children who are brought up in institutions. Comparative studies have shown that although the latter are properly fed, clothed, and kept warm, and although there is an attentive house mother, the average age at which they sit up, crawl, walk, and run for the first time is older than with babies in normal homes. Institutionalized children lack encouragement, and consideration for their individual personalities and feelings. Later, they show their lack of a firm foundation for friendships and dealing with others, by being shallow in their attitudes towards each other and to visitors alike. This is a *tendency*, not an inevitable pattern: there *are* institutions where there are people who can act as mother-substitutes rather than nurses. But the evidence for 'long-stay personality' is very considerable. (Maureen Oswin's work is recommended for further information on this problem.)

Apart from long-stay in hospital, a serious interruption to a young child's development can be caused by a short visit—in certain circumstances. Under the age of five, all efforts should be made for the mother *to go into hospital with her child.* The principle of this has been fought for, mostly successfully, by the National Association for the Welfare of Children in Hospital (NAWCH). They can advise if a mother encounters heavy opposition from hospital authorities.

The next best thing to going in with a child (who may need to be admitted for observation, or for a minor operation, for example) is to establish unrestricted visiting, and to make sure of being at hand when her baby is prepared for an operation, or is due to regain consciousness after anaesthetic. These are arguably the times when the hospital experience is most frightening. The point of all this is that the effects of alarm are not limited to the time in hospital, or even to a short period after return home. The mother-child relationship has received a sudden and (to the baby) inexplicable rupture. For a fuller account see James Robertson's work, or *Children Apart*, which I wrote under the name Peter Rowlands.

Another thing that can go wrong (*strictly* from the baby's viewpoint) is the arrival of a brother or sister. The standard ways of reducing the shock and displeasure that this will cause him are to bring him well into the secret, as something exciting for all the family, well before the event; to hand a special present to him immediately the arrival makes his first appearance in the home; to increase the time that father devotes to him, and to set aside certain periods of the day which are sacroscanct, for the mother to talk and play with him, and him alone. But some envy and jealousy is *inevitable*. The closer they are in age, the greater the chances of them competing for attention over the same thing, at the same time. This does not of itself do them so much harm as the possible by-products, which are:

(a) that either child is made to feel so guilty about his natural resentment that he suppresses these feelings, which then become extreme;
(b) that one is favoured to the exclusion of the other;
(c) that one hits the other rather too hard.

The commonest mistake is perhaps to assume that children under three—or under seven, for that matter—share the more sophisticated reactions that adults feel when one small child has his 'own' toy snatched away, or when, in retaliation, the other gives him a bleeding nose. 'Unfair' is a concept that is only subjective at this age. Expecting adult morality encourages guilt, and anxiety about feelings that a child cannot keep under control. Sharing time between them, being an intermediary, and separating them before disaster strikes is more practical and more realistic.

Every sensitive parent must feel at some stage that her two small children are *peculiarly* horrible in their relations with each other. The idea that jealous wrangling might be normal—which, unless it is continuous, and unrelieved, it is—cuts little ice. The moments when they seemed to get on charmingly well with each other are forgotten. But relations between young brothers and sisters *do* improve. They often seem to play better together, or tolerate each other more, when both are feeling well, and wide awake, and when each knows that he has a claim on a certain amount of his mother's time all to himself, regularly and often. Complete absence of jealousy on the part of a child of this age may in fact be a cause for concern: it suggests that normal feelings are either absent, or being abnormally repressed.

It is worth noting, too, that playing together is a rare social accomplishment for children under three, and that this begins only gradually, with play in parallel gradually including more interludes in which a joint activity occupies them both.

Another worry that parents have occasionally is that their child seems to be subject to an exceptionally fierce temper. There are instances where a child works up such a rage that he chokes, and turns blue. A doctor may need to advise on the best ways of pacifying such a child—but this is somewhat unusual. Some parents are sharper than others at spotting moments when a tantrum is looming, because frustration is increasing, or for whatever reason. Distraction is much easier before the event, than during it. This course is not always possible. A question then argued in some households is 'Should we give in, and make him happier? Won't this spoil him?'

Allowing a child to associate the merest hint of a tantrum with getting his own way entirely, is to reinforce tantrums, and to leave him totally unprepared for adjustments he will have to make when dealing with other children and other adults. Quite apart from that, many of the things he wants may be dangerous for him. Very often a compromise makes sense: although children may not appear immediately satisfied, they get two messages from this:

(a) that the household is not run entirely on points of principle, and that you are prepared to discuss, adapt, and negotiate, when he feels strongly;
(b) that, all the same, there are some limits beyond which you cannot be budged.

Sometimes, infuriatingly, small children of two or three take special delight in 'exploring the borders' of what is acceptable and what is not. It secures attention, for one thing, but it also gives them a clearer picture of what your limits are. A child will be happier to know you *have* limits, and knowing them makes you an easier target for his imitation. In his eyes, you are *the* person: imitation often seems the goal of life.

But there are times when tantrums accumulate, however quick you are to discern his mood and take avoiding action. He is 'going through a bad patch'. Well, most children do, at some stage. Is he getting enough sleep? Is he missing out on playtime with mother or father, that he had before? A cold, indigestion, or teething trouble can make things worse for him. Is he reflecting an anxiety that his *parents* have—that is, are *you* seriously worried, and do you show it? Do you feel sometimes that he desperately wants to do something—talking, imitating his father, or doing something as well as an older brother—that is just beyond his grasp, and therefore a nagging frustration?

All these questions are worth asking, in case they provide a clue that makes life easier for him and the family. Another point to ask yourself is—do many of his tantrums have something to do with rules and regulations that simplify your work slightly, but have no real importance? Insisting on meat before pudding, and no going back afterwards, is an example of a regulation dictated by convention, but which has no importance for diet whatever, and may be an unnecessary source of annoyance.

While there may seem a large number of problem areas, both physical and mental, the child who is given a great deal of love and attention by his mother during his first three years has an enormous chance of missing most of them, and of surmounting those that crop up. She will be watching out for danger signs, but be entirely positive in doing things with her baby, and helping him along. A baby who is kept interested by his mother has very little time for problems.

Chapter ten

How thinking develops

It is not too early to start considering how a child learns to *think*. Of course what we usually mean when we talk about thinking is a long way off. Working out the answer to a mathematical problem, or sifting evidence to decide the best action to take is not to be expected from this age group. But the seeds of these kinds of thinking are certainly sown in infancy. Understanding how some children go on to become particularly good at certain types of thoughtwork must start with examining the seeds.

The most systematic work done in this area is that of Piaget, the great Swiss psychologist. He and his colleagues devoted their life's work to observing children of all ages, and noting down in great detail how they reacted to problems or difficulties of different sorts. He was able to distinguish on the basis of this evidence, successive types of thought processes that followed each other as children grew older. He devised tests that would show whether or not individual children had reached each stage of thought process that was represented by each of them. This meant he would refine his theories of how thinking developed, and he could try them out. Since his tests involved *doing things*, rather than 'knowing' the right words or numbers to play back, they are less open to the charge that they were simply assessing particular knowledge, and not mental approaches to problems.

Piaget noted the reflexes with which a baby is born. These were discussed in Chapter 2. Gradually some of these were adopted and improved on by habit, on the principle of trial and error. Sucking is an example. Others disappeared because they were superseded by other movements which were learned as the brain and the rest of the central nervous system matured sufficiently to organize them. Certain *habits* were gradually formed, i.e. ways of moving and reaching to accommodate to a known or a new stimulus.

During the fifth month, Piaget observed that a certain connection could be made by a child between an instrument and an object that could be obtained by using the instrument. He used an apparatus which presented a baby with a rattle within range of his hands, once the baby has pulled on a cord. The cord's position could be varied: the baby would turn, use it, and obviously expect the rattle to appear again. There was nothing very sophisticated about the mental connection made between the two objects. The cord could be regarded simply as a 'magic provider of rattles'.

This develops into ability to discriminate between different functions that different instruments can be made to fulfil. From six months onwards, a baby will come to learn that the cord can bring the rattle when it is hanging from a pulley, but that when it is flat on the floor a small walking-stick can be hooked into another stretch of cord to get the pulley system working again. In general then, the baby can now assemble a repertoire of behaviour from which to choose the right means to an end according to what he perceives around him. This is a *gradual* development, for obvious reasons. But the baby's thought processes are unlikely to be ready to start it before six months of age.

It is one thing to be able to choose an instrument, and to do something with it from a learned repertoire, but another to find out some new materials within range, to see a new object in view, and then *devise a way* of using the new materials so as to obtain that object. From about twelve months, a baby will do something purposeful (or 'goal-orientated') with the large blunt hook and the small basket he suddenly finds in his playpen. Before, he might have put the hook in his mouth, or picked at the basket, to feel what is was like. Now, seeing an apple outside, beyond the range of his arm or the hook by itself, he is capable of seeing how to fit the hook through the hole in the side of the basket, and swing the apple-catching machine he has made so that the basket traps the fruit and draws it towards him.

It should be noted that these last two developments are closely connected with the course of visual skill. As a reminder, Table 1 shows that from six months on a child is likely to be able to watch complex movements in the room; and he makes for objects with increasing accuracy. At one year, he uses his eyes to look for what he has dropped.

Thinking power and visual skill are so closely wound up with each other that separating them seems rather unreal. The ability (and the assurance) to look for mislaid objects obviously underlies having the idea of seeing what can be done with something in range to get at something out of range.

An element of 'constancy' has entered into the child's thinking at this point. Early in life, out of sight was not only out of mind, it was out of existence—with the exception of mother and what she provided. Later, the wonderful puzzled, intent expression appears on a baby's face which means that he is concerned about something that *was* there but now *isn't*. He may not look for it very much, at first. If he sees it at a distance, or twisted into a new shape, he probably will not even recognize it. But gradually what is called the constancy of objects becomes more and more important, providing both goals and a framework within which to act.

Constancy develops in three broad stages. At first, objects come briefly out of the background, and then sink back into it, without being differentiated. Slowly, they acquire separate identity, but they only exist in so far as the child sees, or handles them, or has recently seen them, and tries to get them back. Eventually, they have existence in their own right—irrespective of where they are, or what has happened to them.

Piaget would not allow the word 'mental' to be used of a baby's first intellectual feats, of the kind described above. They are what he called 'action-schemes'. What he is getting at is that the baby does not make a picture of various objects in his mind, or symbolize them by making models or drawing. He is only dealing with the here and now, with what he can see, can move, and direct towards himself. Nevertheless, in Piaget language, these are the 'cognitive sub-structures' that are the basis for all future perceptual and intellectual work.

Through his second and third year, a child gets better and better at 'action-schemes', bringing new skills into them as he gets stronger, and more accurate in his movements. Some degree of symbolic thinking develops, too. As he begins to understand what is said to him, he will carry out orders in other rooms—such as 'Go and find Teddy', or 'Get me a cup of water, please'. This demands some very simple mental imagery, because he has to think where Teddy or water might be found. It does not go very far, however. Often a child of this age who cannot find a cup is stumped for a suitable alternative to bring the water back in. Some children may not even recognize 'cups' as being a class of objects: this may be only, in their eyes, those tea-cups that he sees his parents regularly use. Generalization may take longer in some areas than others. It is an essential process, depending on maturation and experience—particularly of talking with parents, and being with other children—that makes it possible for an older child to work out problems that involve substitution of objects with similar purposes in the mind.

Some psychologists have criticized Piaget's theories on the grounds that they assume an essential difference between a child's thinking and an adult's. This is a matter for argument. But the observations he made of what children at different ages can and cannot do are invaluable. His explanations of how and why new feats come into a child's ability command respect, too.

A human being, however, rarely has the opportunity to think in an emotional vacuum. That is to say, you need a warm, quiet corner of a university library, and a mind unaffected by thoughts of promotion, love, envy, or need for more money, in order to achieve it. Some Eastern philosophers seem to make extreme demands of an individual to clear his mind of emotional clutter, before the *real* thinking can begin.

For a child, this is possible sometimes, when you see one totally rapt in concentration on what he is doing, so that he is oblivious to his surroundings and apparently forgetful of the tantrum he had an hour ago. But most of the time, thinking is against a background of emotional change. This colours the conclusions reached—as is obvious when a happy child decides a doll needs to be tucked up and cuddled, or when a listless child feels the same doll deserves a smack. It also colours a child's ability to think at different levels. Piaget was the first, for example, to recognize that observation of *how* a child was tackling his allotted problem, and what was evident from his thoughts or actions of how he was feeling could be as instructive as his ability to solve, or get the answer right. A child in distress would be less efficient, and would tend to regress, or perform at a lower level of thinking than that of which he was normally capable. Similarly, a disturbed child will often do badly at school in terms of performance, although he might be found, through individual teaching, to have an IQ that ought to guarantee success.

It seems right, then, in this chapter, to consider briefly the kinds of emotional tone that can affect thinking, at different stages of development.

The pioneer work in this area was by a psychologist called Bridges, who conducted a large-scale study of children of varying ages, from birth to just over two years. The research involved observing children of different ages for long periods at different times of day, and noting down emotional states. The newborn babies were very simple to characterize: they were either quiet, or excited. Their excitement was undifferentiated until they were a fortnight or so old. Then it was clear that sometimes this excitement could reliably be called 'distress'. The next emotional state to be separated off was 'delight', at about two months. This does *not* mean that children below either of these threshholds do not *feel* distress or delight: it is simply a question of when their observed response is clearly one emotion or another.

These early milestones are easy to accept. Although children vary, the order in which they develop separate responses to different emotions says something about the level of these feelings at particular stages of life, and the importance of communicating them to parents. Biologically, it makes good sense that distress should be signalled clearly, because this must serve to protect the human species.

By the age of six months, other emotions are discernible in the baby's face and in his behaviour. These are 'anger', 'fear', and 'disgust', each of which has obviously developed out of 'distress'. Sometimes these are open to several interpretations: it is perfectly possible to see babies in a state of anger combined with disgust, for instance. Some of Bridges's other categorizations probably owe more to the eye of the beholder: it may take a trained eye to spot the differences between 'joy' and 'delight' for example. But it is worth noting that affection begins to make a clear appearance from about nine months, and jealousy from about fifteen months.

Mothers can read affection in the first eye-to-eye glances they share in their babies' second month. But an observer only notices differences between showing affection and showing delight much later. The concept of affection demands a clear picture of someone outside one's own existence who discerns more than just a smile when it is feeding time. The baby has to learn to incorporate the sense of himself as being different from his mother in his thinking. It is easy for us to assume that he is there, and she is beside him, so he must see the differences. But it needs maturation of the brain as well as experience if the concept of 'self' and 'others' is to be clear. This is the main reason why affection appears separately from delight rather later in the baby's repertoire.

Jealousy demands a particular view of the source of frustration, anger, and distress that a baby is feeling. Again, the concept of 'self' has to be well established first. But the *kind* of source of trouble also has to be identified as a regular nuisance.

These are perhaps the main emotional states that will become apparent during the first years of life. It is easy to see how thinking can become more urgent, more clouded, and how perception can be distorted by each of them. It is a truism to say that 'we see what we expect to see'. An emotional 'set' of, say, anger, will dictate *how* the stimuli of a problem situation are perceived. A helpful word may seem a threat; a toy belonging to a brother becomes a hateful symbol of the object of jealousy. A child who is elated, on the other hand, may interpret what he would normally recognize as dangerous as all part of a delightful scene.

One kind of emotional spur or overtone to thinking is not really covered by this analysis. Observation of very young children shows that there is a distinctive *drive* among some, which is only partially, or occasionally there among others. Intense motivation to explore, seize, and control is characteristic of some babies—to an extent that talking in terms of their all being equal, except for the effects of parental encouragement, does not seem at all adequate. Some of them are described by their parents as being 'very competitive, right from the start'. But competitive with *what*? No baby can know rivalry, until he meets rivals. It is a paradox that some children seem to anticipate the need to be competitive.

Motivation of course varies with change in environment. Children who have been deprived or under-nourished with regard to affection sometimes seem to show particularly high 'need achievement' as they grow older: this is as if success, whether in academic, artistic, or physical terms, is a necessary compensation for them. But the original level of motivation, and the way in which it develops in constant conditions, are factors that we do not sufficiently understand. Some children seem to be specially endowed with high motivation, and this is reflected in the determination with which they think a problem through.

Most parents will have children of moderate motivation, who will sometimes be interested in tackling something new, and will sometimes be perfectly happy to ignore it, and repeat what they know. You cannot *make* a child more interested in using his mind, and history is full of examples of unpleasant results of expecting too much from young children. The prime requirements of a young child, for him to develop his intellectual potential seem to be these:

(a) A very warm loving atmosphere, at the core of which is a very tight bond of affection between him and his mother (or mother-substitute).
(b) Being encouraged to try something new, but not having new ideas thrust upon him. Showing interest in what he does, and how he vocalizes, and applauding when he grasps and does something with a new toy, is much more important than providing any new toys at all.
(c) Talking with him (rather than *to* him). Even when traffic seems mostly one-way (i.e. before a baby is vocalizing much) this shows how you value communication, and he will enjoy it and in time do the same. Talking *to* a child is adopting a special precious tone for addressing infants which I am certain (though I cannot prove it) that they all rumble as bogus in the end. It also means ignoring his responses or cutting them off. But singing or chanting nursery rhymes is fine: he will soon join in, in his way.
(d) Changing his stimulation frequently, so that he sees, touches, hears, and plays with different things. (Do not *stop* him from enjoying something he is engrossed in: but equally, don't simply stick a pram out of doors saying 'Fresh air is good for him' without giving him a view more inspiring than that of a wooden fence.)
(e) Allowing exploration. This follows closely from (d). It is a matter of degree and compromise. Of course you do not want a mess everywhere, nor do you want him to seize and destroy an antique clock. But learning to learn and to enjoy it involves finding out what porridge feels like, how newspaper tears and can be pressed into a ball, how the petals of a dandelion can be pulled out, what you can do with mud, what the different parts of your body feel like when you poke at them, and a million other things.
(f) Encouraging independence, without forcing it on him, *or* insisting on particular ways of doing things. Some parents delight in the feeling that their child is so helpless that he depends utterly on them: this retards intellectual development, because it makes it unnecessary for the child to think and learn.
(g) Sharing interests. It is remarkable how a toy which a toddler has briefly considered, then abandoned, suddenly acquires magical attraction when his father is seen on hands and knees, trying to

make it work. Contests *and* co-operative ventures in building huge Lego bridges, in making Spirograph drawings, in getting Hotwheels toys to go the furthest distance, or simply in colouring pictures, all increase pleasure in projects, and confidence in one's own ability.

(h) Some children have a perceptual handicap. Whether this is in sight, hearing, or the ability to organize sensory input in the brain, an important aid to mental development is practice at using more than one sense to discover more about life round about them: this means being encouraged to feel, smell, and hear objects as well as see them, and name them.

One idea that is often current is that children who follow the firstborn must have an advantage in intellectual progress. The presence of a slightly older child who is learning toilet training, speech, and all kinds of games, is supposed to increase motivation to master these things, as well as offering an example to copy. The argument sounds convincing, but the *results* in terms of children's achievements do not actually bear it out. Research in the last decade among thousands of children points to an advantage in achievement at the primary school level to the firstborn (or only children), and sometimes to the youngest child in the family—where there are more than two.

This suggests that although copying an older brother or sister must play a part in development, it is very small by comparison with *the amount of attention received from parents, and mother in particular.*

114 How thinking develops

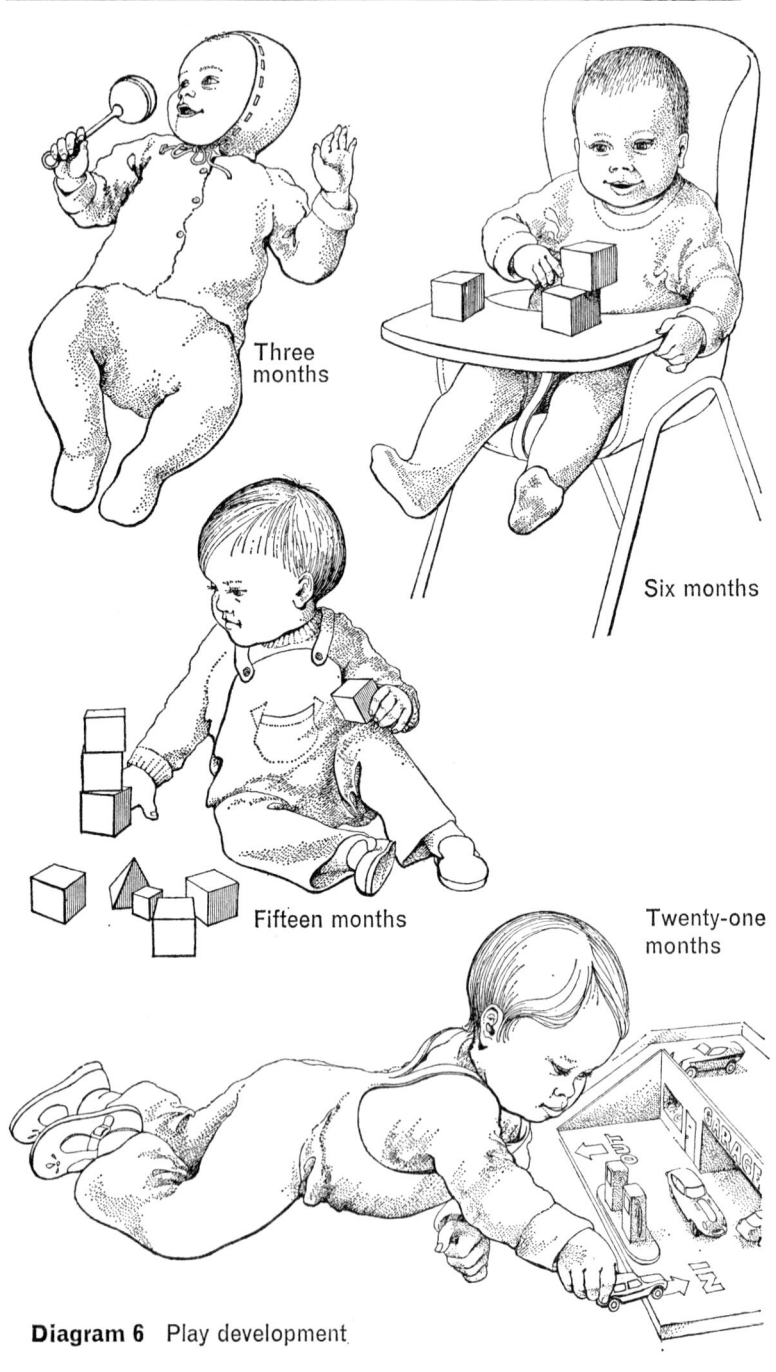

Three months

Six months

Fifteen months

Twenty-one months

Diagram 6 Play development

Chapter eleven

Two years old and beyond

By the time a baby reaches two, his parents may expect him to have developed in each of the following ways:

More mobile, more of the time He moves fast, usually but not necessarily on his hind legs. He gets round the house more, too, looking for people and things that he remembers might be around. It is sometimes as if he is reminding himself of the geography of his home, and of the activities that he has observed in particular spots—mother working in the kitchen, father in the study, or, nowadays, vice versa. His sleep need has declined rapidly, so that he may wake at about seven, and be difficult to keep in his nursery until the rest of the household is up and about, despite stubbornly refusing to sleep in the evening until half-past-six or later. Whether he needs or wants a nap in the afternoon depends very much on the child. But no nap means a very fragile temper by tea-time. On the other hand, a deep sleep which is allowed to go on for two hours may mean repeated visits later to quiet an ebullient nightbird. Each mother will have to judge what her own compromise should be, but a quiet half-hour after lunch, with music or a story often seems best.

Eating more 'normal' food He eats much more of the family's normal meals—with obvious exceptions, such as the special sausages that father likes, and difficult vegetables like onions and leeks. When a mother cannot be bothered to chop up small what the rest of the family is eating, she may fall back on the occasional tin of prepared baby food—but with a good mixer she can achieve the same result very simply, more cheaply. Nowadays, what tends to happen is that in the interests of simplification, father's spiced sausages disappear from the menu, while frozen fish products, and baked beans, come in more and more often, because everybody will eat them. This is all right, provided everyone *enjoys* these products: it is pointless antagonizing father by making him feel he has to suffer because of the baby.

More independent This includes self-service at mealtimes (at least, to *start* with), and sometimes insistence in doing part of his own dressing or undressing. He may have a good idea of how to behave on his potty, and may be successful a lot of the time at knowing when to find it or summon aid. It may also extend to stubbornness, and a negative phase, in which suggestions meet with a uniform 'No'—a word which the child has come to respect as having magical properties that need careful exploration.

More original He may have used his teddy-bear conventionally up till two years. It was taken into bed, hugged, and perhaps wrestled with. There might have been some make-believe feeding, too. Around two, there are many more purposes, a child decides, to which a teddy-bear might be put: he can be put in the bath and scrubbed, put into the oven to cook, put into orbit via the window. Nor does a teddy-bear need to keep its essential features. A strong two-year-old may pull out his eyes, or tear open a seam, to examine his stuffing. This is what imagination does, and although it is often painful to behold, this is in a way what toys are for. They provide exploratory material for games which show him 'What would happen if . . . ?' and a release for aggression as well as curiosity drive. He will be more recognizably constructive (although there is little real difference between constructive and destructive imaginative play in a child of this age) with toys and household objects with which he learns he can imitate what parents are doing. A two-year-old may well sneak a saucepan from the kitchen and fill it with a strange 'soup' of wooden blocks, beads, plastic triangles, Lego pieces, etc., and enjoy this as a culinary exercise.

More of an individual personality When one-year-olds are seen in the same room, one or two of them may stand out from the rest as individuals who are clearly different. The others look much of a muchness—except to their mothers, of course. The same is not true for any group of children of two years or above—with the exception of special groups, such as those who become more stereotyped through living in an authoritarian institution.

Two-year-olds display all sorts of character traits. Many of them are still fragile traits, however, that disappear once the child comes under any emotional pressure. A pioneering, self-assertive two-year-old, for instance, may seem extremely different once his wishes are thwarted, or he becomes over-tired. But there are many ways in which a two-year-old shows that he has a particular way of meeting a new person, or starting a new problem, or reacting when faced with a difficulty. Those who are late at talking and at walking may

Table 11 Social progress (1–3 years)

Throughout months 13–18	Continuing need for mother's presence: 'clings' to prevent her leaving, 'punishes' her by resisting or ignoring her, demands to accompany her, wherever she goes.
18 months	More competitive with brothers and sisters.
	Imitates many more adult activities: housework, father going to work.
	Helps mother at dressing time, bathtime, etc.
	Enjoys watching other children play, but plays separately.
2 years	Can understand much more than he can express: obeys requests; listens with enjoyment to stories as well as rhymes; becomes acutely observant of being discussed; but, becomes frustrated by inability to make himself understood.
	May start asking a lot of questions.
	May have a strong 'negative' phase: refuses to co-operate.
Throughout third year	Enjoys rituals involving mother, or rest of family.
	Goes through a phase of preferring one parent to the other.
	Tantrums liable at any time. May be aggressive.
	Relates more to other children, but prefers playing in parallel.
	Notices differences between boys and girls.
	More tolerant of mother's absence, but reacts badly to sudden separation.

still be keeping some surprises in store about themselves. The same can be said of children who are to develop strong 'anal personality' tendencies (see Chapter 5), but this is most unlikely among children whose parents have avoided inspiring alarm or guilt during toilet training.

Father's child, as well as mother's As a rule, both a boy and a girl will show considerably more curiosity about the man who beamed at them and cuddled them intermittently, as soon as they can move and follow him round the house. Because he is less predictable, in his comings and goings, he may be the object of more interest. Where there is more than one young child, there will be keen rivalry for his attention. Precisely how a child develops a repertoire of behaviour to gain his attention, and delay his departure from the bedside in the evening, may be a significant element in the development of character mentioned above. Some children will learn to favour a confident approach, some a wheedling approach, some will be coy and others will affect pathos. How the father reacts to various opening moves, and how single-minded he is in showing interest and affection must also affect character development, by the same token.

Those who criticized Tim's mother for having a tea party on his first birthday, may not feel more indulgent towards her for holding one on his second birthday, too. After all, though he may be able to repeat 'bud-day' after his mother, he cannot fully understand the concept. But he shares her pleasure in the idea, and he already has a sense of occasion.

Tim

He is still a slow walker. He does not enjoy being on his legs for any length of time, although sometimes he will stand at a window-ledge for a few minutes, gazing into the street, watching carefully anything that is going on outside. His mother has seen the doctor; he examined Tim and told her not to worry.

He looks much more dashing than he did a year ago. His sartorial line is not interrupted by the bulge of a nappy any more. He has been clean and dry for three months now—except for two wet nights when he caught a bad cold.

He consents to be led to the door, walking hand-in-hand, to greet the first guest. Frances bursts in, and plants a smacking kiss on his forehead, which makes him over-balance. He looks aggrieved, and stubbornly refuses to get up when Frances tries to haul him to his feet. 'Oh no, Francie!' he tells her. Tim is stubborn, in his way.

'Get up, get up, Tim! Happy birthday!'

His mother wisely picks him up before a fight develops. He is given a present, and he applies himself to unwrapping it. He recognizes a bow, and knows that you pull on one end to undo it. Inside he finds a car, and he addresses it, 'Car!'—with satisfaction.

Frances

She wants to make it work. She takes it from Tim crying 'Car goes—voom! Car goes—voom!', and gets an appropriate noise from the wheels with every 'Voom'. Then she drops it on the floor and rushes past him, making for the living-room. She has played in this house several times, and knows where the toy box is.

This time she sees that the toy box has been pushed to one end of the room, and there are some books and cushions on top of the lid. 'Tim's mummy!' she calls out. 'Tim's mummy! Toys! I want the toys!'

This looks rather blunt and peremptory in print, but coming from Frances, the words contrive to sound charming. She talks a lot for her age, as does Tim, but she is perhaps quicker at *combining* words, which is difficult for a two-year-old. She is quick because she is impulsive, and says words or phrases as she feels she needs them, and as she feels they ought to be like, without working them out. Often she is wrong, but her mother guides her very gently into becoming more accurate. She sometimes adds 'please', at her mother's urging, and uses it because it gets results—but it is a ritual word, without meaning.

Frances has soon got some favourite games to play with. She takes *everything* out of the box, and carefully selects one or two from the display. She enjoys displays, and making grand arrangements of possessions, and she loves the tour of inspection she can make afterwards.

Lesley

Lesley and her mother have entered almost unperceived. Lesley comes in with wide, rather fearful eyes, gripping her mother's hand tight. She looks round in all directions, and seems to sense danger in every corner.

This is the first time she has been brought to Tim's house, which makes her reaction not uncommon. Hearing Frances chattering to herself over the toys gives her no comfort: at this age, the fact that another is having fun inspires very little reassurance.

Then she catches sight of a dog on wheels. She points to it, and whispers, 'Cottie' to her mother. 'Yes, that's a Scottie, just like yours', her mother answers. 'Why don't you go and play with Scottie?'

'Just like yours' is not understood. To Lesley, there is *one* Scottie. And Scottie belongs to *her*. She goes up to the dog, grabs hold of the bar attached to its base block, and steers him back to base.

'Play with doggie!' Frances comes up to her all smiles, with a suggestion of shriek in her voice. What she says is part comment, part command, part request. 'I'll show you', she says—(a more advanced use of personal pronouns than the other children of two can command)—and tries to take over the controls from Lesley.

Refusing to relax her tight grip, Lesley murmurs '*My* Cottie', and there is a moment's confrontation. Lesley has in fact faced this predicament before: she has a younger, nine-month-old sister, who is beginning to encroach on her territory and possessions. She is used to winning.

Fortunately Frances is too excited with the party to continue the brief struggle. She sees Tim has just been given another present, and rushes off to investigate. Lesley takes the dog back to her mother's corner. Her manner suggests she has rescued her regiment's colours from the field of battle.

The two-year-olds do not play together: when they meet it is for demonstrating a learned ritual—as with Frances greeting Tim, or when both are fascinated by a toy, and a both-want-it situation may develop.

Lesley is small, but wiry. She could *probably* move as much and as fast as Frances, but does not normally choose to rush about. She is notable in that she is sharp-eyed, picks out what attracts her, and concentrates on getting it determinedly. Her vocabulary is wide, but seems less advanced than Frances's, because she chatters less in company. She talks to her mother, her toys, and herself. The arrival of her sister unsettled her and put back her toilet training several months. But she has had continuing close attention from her mother, and although she clings more than she might otherwise have done, she does not show much jealousy or disturbed behaviour.

Peter

He has come in with his mother. He seems entirely different from the timid creature who attended the same function last year. He bursts in with a laugh, and surveys the scene. The present and card that his mother put into his hands on the doorstep remain in his clutches as he goes past Tim to see what Frances is playing with. He has to be asked again to give them to Tim. This he does, good-naturedly, but with no sense of occasion.

What he has come for is a 'party', and in the past few months he has been given a wonderful hazy idea of 'party' as being something very exciting. Partly this is from experience gained away from home, but the main influence has been his older brother's delirious joy at celebrating his sixth birthday in style. He had come to a 'party'—not to give presents to Tim. One concept at a time is ample for a two-year-old.

Peter alarms some of the other mothers by pointing his fingers at their children and making 'banging' sounds, as if shooting them. This means nothing, in fact. It is behaviour that his brother considers standard practice—and his brother is on a heroic plane, in Peter's eyes. Peter has no idea what a gun, or what shooting might mean.

They respect Peter more for his skill with a big slate which he finds in the toy box. Very few two-year-olds hold a chalk as Peter does, held between his thumb and his four fingers. In a few months he may even be able to hold it 'normally' between his thumb and his first two fingers. All the others in the room would clutch the chalk in their fists, although they have all just begun to enjoy the feeling of making scribbles and spreading different colours over blackboards or paper. Peter can actually make some representational drawings, which is also advanced behaviour. His 'tiger' is only just about recognizable as a member of the cat family, but it is impressive. The most interesting or alarming parts of the animal are exaggerated in size, as is the case with most children's drawings. The head and the great paws are monstrous, the eyes are like saucers, and the whiskers travel half-way across the slate.

At one he was slow at using his hands. But now he has more than made up for it. His parents approve and encourage him, and his brother's toys and play give him many examples to copy.

His speech is rather rudimentary, however. It seems as if it has developed very little over the year. What progress there is may be masked by the fact that he is rather shy about speaking. When asked a direct question—like many boys between two and three—he loses confidence, and murmurs something that is an underachievement. In fact, he and Tim are true to type in that they are both somewhat behind Frances and Lesley in speech: research shows girls have a slight advantage over boys at this time of life.

Peter and Tim enjoy going to each other's houses. It is known territory. They will even repeat with pleasure what their mothers tell them before such a visit— '——'s house today, mummy!' But when they arrive, they hardly ever even greet each other, although they will glance at what each other is doing. Once or twice they have wrestled over a toy, or about whose turn it is on the low swing in the garden. Somehow, though, there is an indefinable sense that they like each other.

Tim notices that his mother is careful to put away the wrapping paper and string from his presents. When his next present is unwrapped, he ignores the contents, and tries folding up the paper neatly. He still likes to have things done properly. When Frances comes and whisks the paper away, trying to see the present she imagines is underneath, he is cross with her. 'No!' he shouts, and he thumps her on the leg with his fist. Taken aback, Frances cries, and gives Tim a kick. Older children would continue fighting: but these simply howl indignantly, rubbing their wounds aggrievedly, and giving each other black looks.

The other children take very little notice, as the two mothers concerned quickly restore peace, and pacify the combatants. Lesley nudges her mother, and comments to her, 'Babies crying, mummy', with no emotion. Peter turns round from the jig-saw puzzle he is solving, and looks as if to say 'Don't disturb me'.

There is one other child, though, who does feel a bit alarmed at the scene. This is the fifth guest, who needs a special introduction.

Mary

Mary has rounded features, and the effect is emphasized by the fact that although she is two-and-a-half, she is only about as mobile as Tim, and is still wearing a nappy by day. When the howling starts, she is nervous, and clings to her mother. 'Oh-oh!', she cries, and holds on to her coat, making it difficult for her mother to take it off.

But Mary can be quickly distracted, and she has a very cheerful nature. Her mother has brought a well-known rattle with her, and she shakes this happily. One of the other mothers who has not met Mary before, looks at her with curiosity: a *rattle*, at two?

Mary is in fact a mongol. Her features are distinctive, and rather disconcerting at first. Mary's mother is already painfully aware of a few who quickly avert their eyes when she passes them in the street with her push-chair. But Mary's smile, and her laugh, are so open and winning, that those who know her see a special beauty in her.

There are particular books and organizations for helping parents of mongol children. So why is she here? I believe Mary has her place in this book, and a right to her place in the party.

All children need the company of other children. This becomes more and more important to them in their third year. The pre-school years should be full of opportunities to get used to others—what they do, how they play, and what they demand. This learning ought to be gradual. But a handicapped child has a very special need for the company of normal children, because his rate of learning is much slower, and he needs continuous example, and continuous new stimulation. Later, he will be less self-sufficient, and anxious for company.

A normal child should meet the weaker people in the community as well as the stronger ones. Understanding that they exist, and that they have their own ways and their own needs is part of the making of a civilized human being, and it cannot start too young. This is the way to an *integrated* society, which does not despise the weaker ones, or condemn them to living apart, whether they are handicapped or old.

Mary will learn to talk at Frances's level, at about six years. (She is 'high grade'.) She will then learn, also slowly, to read a little, to write a little, to take care of herself, and to do some work which is useful, and in which she can take a pride. She may develop a better sense of rhythm and will dance better than most of them, although at other times she may be clumsy. She will never hurt any of them—unless she trips and falls on one of them. She will love helping them—if they have the patience to let her. She will never share any of their sexual problems, and she will be naughty but will never seriously deceive. She has a good sense of fun too. Let her enjoy the party—invitations may get rare and will become very precious to her and her mother.

All the children are pleased when one of the mothers plays the piano. Peter is surprised, because there are no musical instruments in his house. But he decides it is interesting. He pokes at the keys at the top end of the keyboard, and is quietly discouraged.

When the mothers start singing nursery rhymes, the children are delighted. The more daring ones, who are used to this, Frances and Tim, join in with a good sense of melody but are not always in tune. They are too young for most singing games, but enjoy going through 'Oranges and lemons' in pairs, with their mothers. Frances does not want it to stop, and tries to keep the game going with Peter. A roomful of children like Frances would possibly continue for a while by themselves. But she is a natural organizer and even she has to feel 'on form'.

When the children still have the feeling of the music, they are easily persuaded into a game of pulling up Farmer Giles's turnip, in which one by one, each person adds himself to a human chain, in a long attempt to draw the enormous vegetable out of the ground. At the end, all fall over. There is a lot of laughing, and most of the children think it is very funny—particularly since the mothers have joined in—to see everyone roll over on the floor. But Lesley does not know the game, and is worried by her mother falling back with her: it is a jolt to the stability of her world, and she is relieved when she gets up.

Tim has found a Micky Mouse badge on the floor. A year ago, he would have put it in his mouth, and it would have been dangerous. (Even now, it is a dangerous thing when open, or on the floor.) But he has met pins already, and touches the edge cautiously, with his wrist. His mother feels it should go back to Lesley, to whom it belongs—particularly since Lesley sees it and wants it too. There is a major tantrum, then, unexpected but total. Tim is furious. He cannot say what he feels. He has been excited, and is getting tired, and giving up such an interesting trophy seems an outrage. He kicks and screams, and is wisely removed from the scene.

His mother is quietly firm with her son. Taking him to a quiet room helps. Here they are together, and she can reassure him by her cool presence of mind that the storm must pass. Psychologists believe that young children are usually disturbed by their own tantrums, since the energy they release frightens them. This is why calmness helps most; and why trying to shake a child out of a tantrum, or shouting 'Stop it!' usually makes it worse.

The other mothers are sympathetic. All of their children have had similar tantrums, now much noisier and wilder than at one, and getting rather frequent. Mary has milder ones, but they are bad enough. The third year is a severe tantrum period: probably for several reasons:

(a) Rapidly increasing understanding increases the situations where they can be frustrated.
(b) Desire outpaces the means of getting or doing something.
(c) Although they are getting speech, they are furious at not being able to express quickly and effectively what they feel.

The suspicion that one is being laughed at is also high on the list of tantrum triggers, although this was not a factor in Tim's case this time.

Tim is brought back, sucking his thumb, and not before time tea is served. Lesley refuses to eat anything, because it all seems too strange. Her mother transfers some chocolate biscuits to her pocket, then says 'Look what I've found here!' *These* she will eat.

Peter suddenly jumps down and makes for the door. He has just started to open doors but this one—help!—has a different handle from the ones he can manage. Without a second to spare his mother gets him to the bathroom. Mary and Frances compete to see which can have the messier face. Frances wolfs her food, but only a fraction goes inside her mouth. Mary needs help, but joins in happily, using both hands.

This year, the cake ritual is much more of an occasion. Although Tim has been given a vague idea that there are *two* candles, and he is *two* years old, these are mere words to him. None of the children has any concept of numbers as yet. This is something that some of them may start developing in the year to come. But the lighting of the candles is magic, and is treated as such. There is competition to blow out the match. They have picked up some of the words of the ritual song, too. It is unintelligible, but fun. Tim obeys instructions, but his first blow is explosive rather than effective. When he gets it right, he is delighted.

The party is a success, despite fights, tantrums, and one or two near-accidents. But it depends for its success on the mothers being there, and on their being contributors.

Most of the developments in the third year have been outlined already. But there are some which still need to be discussed.

The first is the point that neither a two-year-old nor a three-year-old has very much idea about what is real and what is fantasy. They are exploring the differences, slowly. They are liable to accept anything that they *want* to be real as real. They cannot actually lie, because that would assume that they knew clearly what the truth was. Often older brothers and sisters will laugh at or protest at the distortions or fantasies that the young ones produce. Sometimes even parents show displeasure at them. It is rather like demanding that a two-year-old should stifle his imagination.

Two-year-olds often talk to their teddy-bears or dolls as if they were real. They talk to imaginary toys, too. Sometimes it seems as if they are testing out their new-found language skills. You can discern their pleasure in repeating phrases they have heard, appositely or not. Sometimes they seem to be talking as if in imitation of the tone used by their parents to themselves. Sometimes they are going over various incidents of the day in their own terms, as if they are trying to understand them properly by re-living them, or embroidering them in a story. A two-year-old girl I know observed her mother bringing home a five-day-old brother from hospital. She was allowed to watch the nappy-changing, a stage the girl had already left behind. She then got flannels and hand-towels from the bathroom and arranged them on her furry animals, her dolls, and even the cat curled up on the settee. This was her exploration of the new event. Most of the elements discussed about reality are apparent in her behaviour—plus a need to come to terms with incipient jealousy.

Between two and three the pangs of jealousy are very real. Often this results in regressive behaviour. (This happened with Lesley, who stopped trying to organize her visits to the potty when it was obvious to her that a tiny creature who always needed her nappy changed got more attention.) Other regressive signs can be whining, crying, lolling about on chairs and beds, refusing to talk or understand requests, and loss of learned self-feeding behaviour. But it all passes, particularly if it is understood by a parent for what it is—*not* naughtiness, but a cry for help. Compromises must be found between the demands of each child, and where there is plenty of love compromises emerge.

A child may decide to be entirely negative for a while, revelling in the use of the word 'no'. He is trying out his power as an independent unit. A negative child is often one who has not been given a complete chance to try to be independent earlier. Again, this phase passes.

Self-exposure sometimes presents problems for parents. But these problems are really of the *parents*' making, not the child's. Is there anything more natural than to show off your body, if you happen to be proud of it? This is particularly so, if you have just started to discern differences between the sexes. Like masturbation (see the answer to question 6 in the Appendix to Chapter 8) it can be embarrassing although most people nowadays are more likely to be amused or at least tolerant. Distraction works far better than prevention.

Up till the age of two, disturbance in the night could be for any reason. Once a child can talk about it—even when half-asleep—it is easier to be precise about what happened. We do not know for certain when children start to dream, except by inference from EEG recordings of sleep rhythms, which are open to question, as brainwave patterns during dreams vary to some extent between individuals. But a two-year-old can tell you he has had a nightmare. One informed me once that he had dreamt of 'tomatoes rolling downhill at me'. He had woken up, screaming. Less than a week before, he had had a gastric upset, and been ill. If a young child has a nightmare it is usually because he is worried about something, and it is worth considering what it might be. Some psychologists feel this is usually fear of one's own temper, and its effects.

Many two-year-olds like rituals. (Tim is a good example.) Others seem to want life to be haphazard, but even these expect certain things to be in place at certain times. Resistance to change can be formidable. A major change, such as moving house, can be very disturbing at this age, and a careful introduction to the new house, showing familiar possessions comfortably settled in a new nursery, is important.

Sometimes they may seem intolerably egotistical—always concerned about what is 'mine!', what 'I want!', etc. When, you may ask, will they start becoming kind and considerate, and when will they stop thinking that taking turns is a means of deceiving them? The answer is that although for the time being they may seem first and foremost a selfish organism, they are gradually taking cues from their parents about other feelings. They stroke a new baby's head, they pat the dog, they even, still at two, come up and say 'Poor mummy's tired'. This is the start. They are copying, rather than feeling moved by the pathos of the baby's innocent helplessness, or mother's worried frown. But they are noting kindnesses all the time, and—assuming they have a solid bond of love and mutual interest with their parents—they will soon come to repay these kindnesses out of a real desire to do so.

Further reading

Here is one very helpful book, to be consulted especially when worried about something going wrong.

Jolly, Hugh, *The Book of Child Care,* Allen & Unwin, 1975.

Here are some books which would be worth looking at, for anyone who feels prompted to make a closer study of children's development. An asterisk beside the name of a book indicates that it is considerably more demanding for the average reader.

Bowlby, John, *Child Care and the Growth of Love,* Penguin Books, 2nd edition, 1965.
Bowlby, John, *Attachment and Loss,* vol. I, Hogarth Press, 1969; Penguin Books, 1971.
Bowlby, John, *Separation: Anxiety and Anger,* vol. II, Hogarth Press, 1973.
Brierley, John, *The Thinking Machine,* Heinemann, 1973.
Foss, B. M. (ed.), **Determinants of Infant Behaviour,* 4 vols, Methuen, 1969.
Griffiths, Ruth, *The Abilities of Babies,* University of London Press, 1967.
Hunt, J. M., *Intelligence and Experience,* New York: Ronald Press, 1961.
Illingworth, R. S., *Babies and Young Children,* Churchill, 1968.
Illingworth, R. S., **The Development of the Infant and the Young Child: Normal and Abnormal,* (5th ed.), Livingstone, 1972.
Klein, Paul, **Fact and Fantasy in Freudian Theory,* Methuen, 1972.
Oswin, Maureen, *Empty Hours: Weekend Life of Handicapped Children in Institutions,* Allen Lane, 1971.
Piaget, J., **The Origins of Intelligence in the Child,* Routledge & Kegan Paul, 1953.
Robertson, James, *Young Children in Hospital,* Tavistock, 1970.

Rowlands, Peter, *Children Apart: Problems of Early Separation from Parents,* Dent, 1973.

Sheridan, Mary D., *Children's Developmental Progress*, NFER Publishing Co., 1973.